PRAISE FOR RESTORING THE BROKEN PLACES...

"*Restoring the Broken Places* is true to its promise and takes the reader on a journey of transformation. With deep thoughts, practical steps to walk out, and God's Word as the foundation, Becky's book is an excellent resource for those in need of giving or receiving forgiveness. We all face this dilemma, and Becky helps us figure out how to emerge victoriously from this battle."

~Amy Elaine Martinez, Founder: Amy Elaine Ministries and Real Victory Radio

"In *Restoring the Broken Places*, Becky Cortino has captured the true essence of forgiveness—the bondage it creates and the freedom we experience when we follow the mandate in Scripture to forgive as we have been forgiven. Becky has learned firsthand the power of forgiveness and shares that wisdom with the reader."

~Andrea Merrell, freelance editor, and author of *Praying for the Prodigal* and *Marriage: Make It or Break It*

"Undeserved pain strikes us all. When unkind words or unwanted deeds hurt us, we choose whether we will move away from anger and walk toward healing. But how do we restore the broken places in our lives, especially when the grace needed to forgive deep wounds is so costly? Through biblical wisdom, thoughtful questions, and practical applications, Becky Cortino serves as an experienced guide on our journey to transformation."

~David Brannock, Pastor, Writer, Counselor, Greeneville, Tennessee

"Becky Cortino's *Restoring the Broken Places* goes a lot deeper into the spiritual side than most other books on forgiveness. Every chapter is full of scriptural references to back up her points for why it is so important to forgive, let go of resentment without masking the pain, or shortcutting the process to move from a life poisoned with unforgiveness into one set free with grace. If you have been hurt (and who hasn't?), read this book."

~Judy Rodman, Vocal Coach, Writer and Host of All Things Vocal blog & podcast

"Everyone has been injured in some fashion by others, and if we want to enjoy the abundant life God has planned for us, we need to forgive them. But sometimes that is more difficult than expected. *Restoring the Broken Places* takes you through the steps needed to attain ultimate biblical forgiveness."

~ Susan Neal RN, MBA, MHS, Health and Wellness Coach, and Author of *7 Steps to Get Off Sugar and Carbohydrates*

"True forgiveness is a process—a journey and not a destination. There is such a misunderstanding of what forgiveness is. It begins with a decision. But until a person explores the depth and breadth of how they were wounded, in a safe, trusting relationship and environment, the full measure of healing that comes from making a decision to forgive isn't reached. We just go through the motions. The splinter is still there. Somehow being able to forgive others of those tremendous hurts and consequences relieves some of the pain within the soul to find forgiveness for one's self, which is a much more difficult task. And then the journey continues, with a daily grace of a lifestyle of forgiveness."

~Debbie Haynes, Founder, Safe Harbor, Hickory, North Carolina

RESTORING THE BROKEN PLACES

IN AN UNFORGIVING WORLD

BECKY CORTINO

LivRad

Restoring the Broken Places in an Unforgiving World

Copyright © 2020, 2022 by Becky Cortino

Published by LivRad Publishing

905 US Highway 321 #215, Hickory, NC 28601

www.LivRad.com

LivRad: Encouraging Words for Hurting Hearts

First Printing 2020, Second Printing 2022 / Printed in the United States of America / Restoring the Broken Places/ Becky Cortino

ISBN: 9798691998171 ASIN: BO8KFNWVST

ISBN: 978-0-9799093-4-4 ISBN 978-1-6780-5853-1

ISBN: 978-1-6780-5068-9

All rights reserved. No part of this publication may be reproduced, stored in a retrieval system, distributed, or transmitted in any form or by any means – for example: electronic, photocopy, recording – without prior written permission of the publisher. The only exception is brief quotations in printed reviews. Requests for permission must be addressed to Becky Cortino and sent to the above physical mailing address.

Unless otherwise indicated, Scripture quotations are from The Holy Bible, THE MESSAGE. Copyright (C) by Eugene H. Peterson 1993, 1994, 1995, 1996, 2000, 2001, 2002. Used in keeping with NavPress permission and terms of use.

This book is intended to provide helpful insight based on biblical truths on the subject addressed. Readers should seek professional care and assistance in any cases risking personal safety, matters involving security, legal, financial or health-related issues. The author and publisher of this book expressly disclaim responsibility for any and all adverse effects, liability, loss, or risk, personal or otherwise, which is incurred as a consequence, directly or indirectly, arising from the use of and/or application of any of the contents and information contained in this book.

This is a work of nonfction. Incidents and certain examples cited are included for the express purpose of illustrating points made throughout this book. Names and details have been changed to protect the privacy of individuals involved.

DEDICATION

To my mother with love and heartfelt gratefulness for teaching me to write, and so many other wonderful things.
To Pat, thank you for loving. Always.
My heart hurts. My heart soars.
I'm grateful. Thankful. I count it all Joy!
All things are possible.

CONTENTS

Introduction — xi
St Francis of Assisi Peace Prayer — xv

1. Where Restoration Begins — 1
2. Three Undeniable Truths — 15
3. Forgiving Me — 35
4. Forgiving Them — 47
5. Forgiveness Model — 69
6. Forgiving the Offense — 89
7. Don't Want to Forgive — 113
8. Unforgiving Spirits — 129
9. Loving Beyond the Hard Places — 147
10. Life is a Grace-filled Adventure — 159

The Lord's Prayer — 175
Acknowledgments — 177
About the Author — 179
Also By Becky Cortino — 181

INTRODUCTION

Writing this book has been a blessing, a joy, and a hard-won labor of love. Some days the words flowed. Some days I sat back in awe of the truths these words speak to listening hearts. I was deeply touched in how I believe the Lord speaks to us through careful study and serious contemplation of His Word. To illuminate the way in our forgiveness journey, readers will find numerous Scripture references throughout this book.

I prayed my way through every step of writing this book. My hope and prayer is presenting readers a clear understanding of forgiveness. When we know what true forgiveness is, we can apply its principles more effectively. As we extend grace, we experience a supernatural release from relentless pain that has held us captive for far too long. Once we are freed from that bondage, we can live life forward in love.

In the process of my research and writing, I was often surprised by what I learned. Like many, I may not find every aspect of forgiveness personally appealing. As Christians, we are mandated to embrace the practice of forgiving others ongoing in its entirety, not just applying the parts we like best.

Some days I was literally in tears reviewing moving stories shared, remembering those in incomprehensible situations, unceasing pain expressed. Sometimes I cried in recalling a glimpse of incredible courageousness witnessed in those private moments hurting hearts shared with me.

Tears spilled from a heart overflowing with gratefulness for being blessed beyond measure with this book project I never dreamed I would write. Amidst the challenge of presenting the case for forgiveness, I realized in the writing that the Lord had prepared and equipped me to write this as part of His plan for my life.

Writing this book has been the most difficult project I have ever undertaken. I've been writing (and published) since before graduating high school, so I've written for all forms of media (print, broadcast, digital) for a long time. The topic of forgiveness is hard to discuss. Forgiveness covers a vast landscape of human conditions. Thinking about it is incredibly uncomfortable. I was astonished when strangers freely shared personal pain and their experiences with me.

I have listened to many stories of forgiveness and grace. Throughout the telling, I have been blessed as I am reminded of the healing power that touches all lives involved in this sacred act.

I listened patiently to everything shared with me, knowing most of the personal advice or special insight about forgiveness differed from what I found directly in Scripture through my research and study. Even so, I thought it was important to take in the viewpoints as well as the beautiful stories. In my listening, I realized people needed to be heard. They sought affirmation and understanding in a perceived safe place, through a meeting of caring hearts and minds.

I have listened respectfully to many explaining what forgiveness was all about (according to my confidante's view). Sometimes they would impart a word for me to include in this book. I listened with a gentle, quiet presence. I never passed judgment, spouted my opinion, nor showed them where they were wrong about forgiveness, based on my deep-dive study of Scripture.

In the listening, I was inspired by beautiful forgiveness stories.

INTRODUCTION

These divine appointments provided different perspectives, showing me aspects to address in this book. I'm prayerful those who want to know more about forgiveness will read this book because it lays out the case for forgiveness based on Scripture. It explains what grace is and why it is an essential part of life.

Before cultivating a better understanding of what forgiveness is and learning to effectively extend grace, I admit sometimes applying the world's ways to troubling relational situations. I quickly discovered those ways don't work because the problem was never resolved. The incessant pain remained and often grew worse. In my observation, it doesn't seem the world's ways are working for anyone.

Are you still stuck in the middle of a messy problem you'd like to see repaired? If you join me on this journey along the road to forgiveness, I'll share with you what I've learned and show you how to be freed from the pain so you can live forward in love, enjoying God's best for your life.

How to Use this Book

Throughout my writing of this book, I have been abundantly blessed to hear amazing forgiveness stories of inspiring people I have encountered on the journey. They freely shared their deepest, darkest experiences and innermost hearts with me. Each story inspired new dimensions to this book. I respect their privacy and have altered the details of their stories or considered their view as *typical* stories to share with you. Their experiences serve as mile markers along this road we travel together as we make our way toward forgiveness.

In order to get the most out of what I share, readers are advised to release every preconceived notion, long-held belief, and any personal understanding about forgiveness. It is critical to approach this topic with an open mind.

Throughout this book, I have included biblical references, serving as the scriptural basis for what I've written. Readers are encouraged to refer to these passages, reading and studying around each, for a deeper, more personal meaning. As you read, I recommend using a journal to record notes, insights, and Bible verses that speak to your heart—for later review.

All quoted Scripture is taken directly from *THE MESSAGE*. I chose to incorporate this version of the Holy Bible for three reasons:

1. I believe the wording is exceptionally clear, with little room for misunderstanding or misinterpretation.

2. For those unaccustomed to this version of the Bible, I pray you will read God's Word presented in this new way, perhaps receiving a fresh perspective. Scripture references are sprinkled throughout this book as additional resources to allow readers to read and study in their preferred version of the Holy Bible.

3. Scripture references are included because they provide us all valuable instruction on living our best life based on Jesus' example.

Register Your Book Purchase to Receive Special RESTORING Reader Resources!

Reader's Guide to this book, Forgiveness Bible Verse Guide and Bible Verse Cards, Forgiveness Inspirational Music Playlist and More Reader Perks (You will find the link to register your purchase inside this book).

ST FRANCIS OF ASSISI PEACE PRAYER

Lord, make me an instrument of your peace:
    Where there is hatred, let me sow love;
    Where there is injury, pardon;
    Where there is doubt, faith;
    Where there is despair, hope;
    Where there is darkness, light;
    Where there is sadness, joy.

O Divine Master, grant that I may not so much seek
    to be consoled as to console,
    to be understood as to understand,
    to be loved as to love.
    For it is in giving that we receive,
    it is in pardoning that we are pardoned,
    and it is in dying that we are born to eternal life.

ONE
WHERE RESTORATION BEGINS

Getting Real

Hurts we endure can grow to have tremendous influence over us, even with little nurturing. Replaying events as an endless loop in our minds permits them to take over life. As if we opened the door welcoming in unwanted hurt, it promises to always stay near us. By granting permission for it to stay, we allow it precedence in our lives to transform into a deeper, more profound personal pain.

Like an unwelcome visitor choosing to take up residence with us, hurt demands increasing time, space, and attention we don't want to give. Eventually, it becomes a dead weight we dread dragging with us everywhere. This burden makes our every step increasingly labored.

Growing weary, we miss the ease enjoyed before our constant companion began shadowing us. Through a tearful blend of sentimentality for what we believe we've lost and hopeless anguish for what has taken heartless control over life, we enter into a daunting expedition to discover what happened to bring us to this terrible place.

We may never understand why something played out as it did,

but we do know it occurred, bringing relentless pain with it. We cannot alter history, but we can change how we deal with things that happened to us. The answer lies in forgiveness. We can free ourselves of our torment, living victoriously through Jesus Christ by fully embracing this scriptural principle.

Forgiveness is where hope is found. It is a starting place. It is always the beginning of all that is yet to come and all that will be. It is the way to a better life. Be open to accepting the gift. What are you afraid of? Lay your cares, concerns, and fears at the feet of Jesus Christ. He wants to hear from you. He wants to help you. He's waiting for you.

The Bible says in Revelation 3:20-21:

Look at me. I stand at the door. I knock. If you hear me call and open the door, I'll come right in and sit down to supper with you. Conquerors will sit alongside me at the head table, just as I, having conquered, took the place of honor at the side of my Father. That's my gift to the conquerors!

Change Your Mind, Change Your Heart

Any alteration in our way of doing things in life requires a real change of heart to assure a better chance of success. Think about that for a moment. Any change we desire to make in our lives—whether physical, emotional, spiritual, or relational—requires our heart to be different than before.

We take the necessary steps to accomplish our heart's desire, willing to accept a new reality. Any change needed to restore a relationship with others mandates reshaping our hearts too. When we change our way of thinking, our heart is sure to follow. All this is possible through God only, not relying on our own feeble wit, weak spirit, shaky knees—or else this would've already happened by now, right?

James 4:6 reminds us:

You're cheating on God. If all you want is your own way, flirting with the world every chance you get, you end up enemies of God and his way. And do you suppose God doesn't care? The proverb has it that "he's a fiercely jealous lover." And what he gives in love is far better than anything else you'll find. It's common knowledge that "God goes against the willful proud; God gives grace to the willing humble."

Here are a few examples of personal battles created by flirting with the world that abound:

•Physical, but also Mental — *The Battle of Self*: Many with weight issues desire to be thinner, with improved physical and mental health. Based on experience, they are convinced attaining this is not humanly possible. They believe the solution to their problem lies in any other means than just eating healthy foods created by God (versus processed by man) is the only way to accomplish this.

•Emotional — *The Legacy of Loss and Abandonment*: Growing up in a troubled home of an affluent family where all physical needs were met, emotional disconnect pervades. The oldest becomes the Golden Child (achiever). Nothing accomplished seems good enough for the parents to tell their child how pleased they are. This blessing is withheld because the parents die without telling the child.

•Spiritual — *Looking for Answers in Hard Places*: A person needing clarity in life arrives at a crossroad. Resulting from misguided decisions, they are at a dreadful impasse in life, seeking ways to get back on the right course. Overwhelmed, they feel immobilized to make decisions for a way out of this bad situation. They owe endless apologies to many people for what they have done.

•Relational — *The Tie that Binds*: Parents who publicly stated over the years a heartfelt desire for their beloved child's future suddenly discover their hopeful expectation isn't turning out as they believed it would. Their world is turned upside down by the child's choices and life decisions. They no longer recognize their child, but now must accept this new person or risk losing further contact.

Overcoming Life's Obstacles in Relationship-building

Based on your feelings at the moment, you may say what you say, but then you'll do what you'll do. Most days, emotions lead us around. Found at the epicenter of our existence, they profoundly influence how we feel, what we think, what we see, and what we say. They shape what we believe to be accurate about ourselves as well as the world around us.

What we feel impacts our emotions and influences our actions. Reaction to something may remain submerged just under the surface for a while or immediately become undeniably evident. It could be said within every emotionally charged belief lies the potential for an equally powerful reaction waiting to happen.

If we're honest, we know emotions have great influence over life. Feelings are granted free-range access throughout the vast playground of our mind. What we feel about something is not always based on fact but personal perception.

Two important factors readily combine for a convincing blend to create relationship-building obstacles: the eye can be easily fooled, and the human emotional state runs counter to logic. An overriding truth remains constant: infertile soil for growing relationships is always found in a life not based on truth.

Let's look at some common relationship challenges caused by not living in truth and love (requiring forgiveness).

Inability to Commit

Inability to fully commit to another in a marital relationship is an emotional roller coaster careening toward a breakdown. Infidelity happens not only through physical means but also through the heart. Emotional affairs are still affairs that can spark physical infidelity.

Addiction to things that divert a spouse's attention away from their partner is another form of cheating by putting the precious thing most desired first. Some things might seem acceptable: dedication to career or work (workaholic), tirelessly serving others as a recognized pillar of the church or community (approval addict), or extreme exercise and fitness training. Other objects of idolatry regarded as unacceptable are excessive drinking, pornography, drug and substance abuse. All these objects can easily serve as a ready mistress or become a lifetime love affair, drawing the willing away from that which is right and true.

Romans 6:6-11 reminds us why we will never be happy living an uncommitted life and need to receive forgiveness:

Could it be any clearer? Our old way of life was nailed to the cross with Christ, a decisive end to that sin-miserable life—no longer at sin's every beck and call. What we believe is this: If we get included in Christ's sin-conquering death, we also get included in his life-saving resurrection. We know that when Jesus was raised from the dead it was a signal of the end of death-as-the-end. Never again will death have the last word. When Jesus died, he took sin down with him, but alive he brings God down to us. From now on, think of it this way: Sin speaks a dead language that means nothing to you; God speaks your mother tongue, and you hang on every word. You are dead to sin and alive to God. That's what Jesus did.

Lying

Lying by omission is a form of telling untruths. There is no such thing as a white lie. A lie is a lie, no matter how someone attempts to sugarcoat it. The words may taste sweet at first, but the bitter center will soon be discovered.

Intentionally misrepresenting something or someone in an untrue way is a lie. Maybe we uttered words with a smile and good intentions, but the cost for lying is ultimately our own expense. It can easily happen; no one would know. To promise prayer support or to cover another in spoken blessing as a gut reaction with no intent to follow up or with real meaning—versus promises poured out from the heart—is an untruth.

Quoting Scripture to justify every thought or action can serve as a visible means to manipulate the sacred to cover unseemly tracks. This perverts the true meaning of God's Word. Prevaricators are known to dress up their stories, hoping to make them more attractive. It's a fact that the more detail a liar adds to their tale, the surer we can be it is a fraudulent fabrication.

Matthew 5:33-37 instructs on speaking words of truth:

And don't say anything you don't mean. This counsel is embedded deep in our traditions. You only make things worse when you lay down a smoke screen of pious talk, saying, "I'll pray for you," and never doing it, or saying, "God be with you," and not meaning it. You don't make your words true by embellishing them with religious lace. In making your speech sound more religious, it becomes less true. Just say "yes" and "no." When you manipulate words to get your own way, you go wrong.

Misrepresenting a Relationship

Putting optics first can misrepresent a relationship. We know it happens and yet hope never to be part of it. But we may be guilty of doing the same thing, only differently. Presenting things in an untrue light is a form of lying.

Here are some everyday examples:

- Politicians pictured with supporters or adversaries carry a message to all who see but will never know the backstory.
- Pulling others in for appearance's sake or purely personal motivations creates a scrubbed, sterile existence captured by a photograph for posterity.
- Misrepresenting emotions as a means of gaining favor or attention is a dark one-way alley.
- Hand-selected imagery to paint a desirable picture is a sign of being more concerned with what others think than living out the truth of an authentic existence in real life.
- Social media and life online make it easy for us to hyper-focus on optics. Dwelling on visuals doesn't leave an enduring legacy in real life.

In Luke 11: 37-41, Jesus tells a Pharisee the importance of living a clean life, versus the appearance of a perfect life:

When he finished that talk, a Pharisee asked him to dinner. He entered his house and sat right down at the table. The Pharisee was shocked and somewhat offended when he saw that Jesus didn't wash up before the meal. But the Master said to him, "I know you Pharisees burnish the surface of your cups and plates, so they sparkle in the sun, but I also know your insides are maggoty with greed and secret evil. Stupid Pharisees! Didn't the One who made the outside also make the inside? Turn both your pockets and your hearts inside out and give generously to the poor; then your lives will be clean, not just your dishes and your hands."

Neglect

Neglect is intentionally living life closed off from others through inattention, ignoring, or outright shunning. Applying extreme control measures with limited communication while exhibiting a lack of emotion makes hiding personal fear, regret, and feelings of vulnerability easy.

Hidden safely behind powerful intimidation that imprisons targets through a constant stream of sarcasm, ridicule, and criticism creates fear. It casts doubt and uncertainty in others. No one dares enter these foreboding gates. This keeps the desired perimeter of (perceived) safety through promised hurt, effectively creating a deep desire to avoid any attempted personal contact with the provocateur.

Neglect is a weak attempt to control life, to form and live it in a way that seems personally easier to handle. The motivation may be to lessen possible anxiety and the inevitable chaos life (and others) can bring. Sometimes this practice provides the fearful ample time and personal space for activity and influence desired to remain private.

2 Corinthians 5:16-20 reminds that we are called to settle our relationships and live free of imposed bondage:

Because of this decision, we don't evaluate people by what they have or how they look. We looked at the Messiah that way once and got it all wrong, as you know. We certainly don't look at him that way anymore. Now we look inside, and what we see is that anyone united with the Messiah gets a fresh start, is created new. The old life is gone; a new life burgeons. Look at it. All this comes from the God who settled the relationship between us and him, and then called us to settle our relationships with each other. God put the world square with himself through the Messiah, giving the world a fresh start by offering forgiveness of sins. God has given us the task of telling everyone what he is doing. We're Christ's representatives. God uses us to persuade men and women to drop their differences and enter into God's work of making things right between them. We're speaking for Christ himself now: Become friends with God; he's already a friend with you.

. . .

If you struggle with nurturing relationships or find yourself making a lot of messes but willing to make life changes, there is hope. There are things you can do to move toward restoration. If a relationship has unresolved issues, or you're allowing your life to be ruled by another who cannot commit to anything outside of their needs, take heart. Conflict resolution isn't always 100 percent possible but granting a pardon and freeing yourself is sure. In cases where direct contact risks personal safety, release from personal bondage and grace can be granted to the perpetrator with prayer. Through Him all things are possible.

There is no secret formula or magic solution, but whenever absolution is sincerely sought, forgiveness can be found even in this unforgiving world. Forgiveness vanquishes a rueful spirit, setting the path right again. Restoration begins where the differences end. Discovering a mutual point of shared heart is the perfect place to start a conversation with those whom you seek to rekindle your relationship.

Resolve or closure of a troubling situation may never be as we thought or hoped for. Life promises us plenty of occasions for disappointment because things turn out differently than we expected. It's important to consider the fact that there are other individuals involved in troubling matters than just *self*.

Resting in our God who has control over all is the only way. He has the big picture view of what is and what is yet to be. Maybe this will turn out better than we could have imagined, or the best possible result never dreamed. This is not the end of our story.

The process can begin anytime, even where we are at this moment. Prayer is an expansive avenue of grace. Pray for the situation, for all involved. Seek God's guidance and His will throughout. By claiming His promises, we can stand firmly on them, letting the Spirit of God move through life and those around us. He will do all the heavy lifting—He's got this. Prepare to be amazed at where and how He leads.

We can easily get overwhelmed and fall into chaotic thinking about what we believe is an impossible task. Wearing ourselves out is a certainty as we carry the weight of unresolved matters. It's no wonder many don't venture much further than our burden's too-short chain permits. The curious thing is once we pray about a situation, things seem to transform. They look and feel different.

Over time, we may be surprised at how we see those we pray for in a new light. By placing our concerns at the feet of our Father, through His son Jesus Christ, we move away from that painful place. We must let go of concern, leaving it with Him, trusting in faith.

Irreconcilable differences can be transformed through grace. We cannot personally reform others, but God can work for the good of all in astounding ways. Since time began, thousands have testified to this life-changing phenomenon running contrary to human nature. This astonishing metamorphosis of the mortal spirit is proof of how God moves forward in powerful ways, working to quell warring factions, disgruntled relatives, fractured friendships, and comfort trauma survivors. Seeing this happen is awe-inspiring. And we know it's God at work.

Seeing Can Be Deceiving

How we view things or approach challenges and situations dramatically impacts life. Addressing life's challenges with a forgiving spirit, in an attitude of grace, affects the outcome of our efforts to make things right and to live the kind of life God has for us. A positive attitude focused not so much on the problem at hand but the road ahead (based on biblical principles), helps set the course to move forward. Resetting our heart and mind to be open to receive the inevitable blessings while being tested—going willingly into the fires of uncertain circumstances—allows us to see things as they really are ... with new eyes.

This reset can reshape our words and actions, possibly leading to eventual resolution. Astonishing transformations can make an incredible difference, even when there is no grace extended nor any clear decision at the time, beyond an initial encounter. A door has been opened, and there is always hope. That door remains open to let the healing begin.

Bless your enemies; no cursing under your breath. Laugh with your happy friends when they're happy; share tears when they're down. Get along with each other; don't be stuck-up. Make friends with nobodies; don't be the great somebody. Don't hit back; discover beauty in everyone. If you've got it in you, get along with everybody. Don't insist on getting even; that's not for you to do. "I'll do the judging," says God. "I'll take care of it." (Romans 12:14-19)

There are some schools of thought purporting forgiveness doesn't have to be granted for small, inconsequential matters. I'm guessing these types of events might include someone cutting ahead of us in a long line, physically bumping into us as they text, some potentially dangerous traffic altercation, or receiving rude treatment. Following this line of reasoning, identifying offending incidents as "small matters" must be left up to an individual's personal discretion—how they see things. This is incorrect thinking because the Bible instructs us to live in forbearance with one another, not prescribing exact situations when we must willingly dispense grace.

In reading Romans 12:14-19 with clear eyes, we see this passage plainly indicates our forgiveness is to be unconditional and available all the time. There is no day, date, or time listed. Fortunately, we don't have to refer to our calendar, some rulebook, scorecard, or app to evaluate every circumstance all day long. Our Father in heaven has made this simple for us. Granting grace may be the hard part but knowing when is not. Forgiveness is to be extended often and always, equally and freely to all.

In circumstances of relational discord (with the exception of rape and abuse), there is always a common ground of shared concern upon which to meet. This mutual point of convergence is where restoration and healing begin. Not everyone will make the journey to that point. Instead, some people will remain hardheaded or too stubborn to admit their need. While their bag may be packed and ready to go, they may never consider joining us on the road to forgiveness. The scenery will be different for everyone, but we share the final destination that lies ahead for those who seek it.

Those who live by personal preference, choosing not to move forward to restore a relational break, directly contradict biblical instruction. No doubt there have been times in life when we've found ourselves making this decision by just walking away. When we accept the mess as is, whatever it may bring in life, we opt to drag it along with us forever.

Because we have the free will to decide doesn't mean we always choose rightly. Making a wrong choice promises continued pain by being eternally lashed to a troublesome situation we long to free ourselves from. We can deny it all and run away, but we can never hide from the truth. The truth must never be avoided, for within the core of a distressing matter a stable foundation for rebuilding a relationship is found.

Beginning the restoration process can be difficult because reviewing a situation is required. It's excruciatingly painful for everyone, including the one who initiated it. Personal truth spoken about the hurt experienced brings an offensive matter into the bright light of reality. A careful examination and expression of offense can be too much to bear. The conversation must be an honest accounting of what happened to cause the hurt, detailing the unnecessary pain suffered as a consequence of the perpetrator's actions.

The wrongdoer may never agree with everything described, but they cannot refute the distress caused. At some point, the instigator of an incident has to recognize how his or her actions created this situation. The truth is the event happened, and its occurrence is credited to the one who brought it about. Opinions and voluntary standards don't constitute the truth. The truth is what is and can never be erased.

Perhaps we finally mustered the courage to make things right. We come to the table. Based on shared concern, we are willing to stand on the solid ground of reconciliation supported by God's Word. We patiently wait. Maybe today we will repair this situation, or the others involved will decide otherwise. We try. We can still release ourselves from its grip and control, even if others are not willing.

Beyond the fact of our own release from this captivity, consider the possibility of what grace looks like to others involved. What if they are not Christians but see us shining in the dark, showing His love? It may cause them to stop and wonder, possibly ridicule, or want some of this peace for their lives as well. What if it turns out we're the only one to show these people forgiveness through our living testimony? No heart is too hard to be penetrated by God.

Scripture reminds us many times that as followers of Christ we have a great responsibility. We have received His grace. Following Jesus' example, we need to extend forgiveness to others. In so doing, we have no promise of reconciliation or ever truly restoring our broken relationship with another—but we can lay the matter at His feet and pray. The issue can be any size, and not even about something that happened to us. We can pray for others, world events, or global crises. Isn't it wonderful we can always pray to a loving God about anything at any time, knowing nothing is too big for Him to handle?

This is going to be trouble on a scale beyond what the world has ever seen or will see again. If these days of trouble were left to run their course, nobody would make it. But on account of God's chosen people, the trouble will be cut short. (Matthew 24:21-22)

Forgiving in Real Life: Apply the Principles and Live these Truths by Prayerful Preparation

Forgiveness is always found where the differences end. Forgiveness begins when we pray and seek it ... and when we receive it. In the process, we become more ready to give it.

Maybe like me, you've tried the world's ways and found they don't work. If you're still stuck in the middle of a mess, it's time to try a new way. Wonderful things happen when our lives and practices line up more closely with Scripture. His ways—not ours—work.

Action step

Pray for the difficult people in your life: wrongdoers, perpetrator(s), troubling situations.

Pray for God's guidance, strength, peace, and His continued protection.

TWO
THREE UNDENIABLE TRUTHS

In my deep-dive study on the topic of forgiveness, three undeniable truths clearly emerged. Because they are foundational, each is worth discussing before we continue further on the road to forgiveness. These three axioms are integral. None are mutually exclusive nor is one more important than the others.

Recognizing the existence of these truths and understanding how they impact forgiveness keeps us on track.

UNDENIABLE TRUTH #1:
There is more Pain, Less Gain without Forgiveness

Life today is filled with more conveniences than ever before in history. They exist to solve problems and make life flow in the process. Devices, appliances, and apps allow us to feel we're accomplishing more things in powerful ways with less time spent. If we're fortunate, this is the case. We strive to live with purpose. There is an incredible rush of personal satisfaction in checking off to-do list items. Seamlessly moving on to the next thing can be addictive.

Based on our desire to move forward and create, it's understandable how quickly we become frustrated when immense amounts of concern, our energy, and our focus are diverted from priorities. We attempt to insulate ourselves to lessen discomfort caused by a troubling issue. If we're not careful, the matter becomes the unintended center of attention, derailing us from advancing.

Life is hard. Forgiving is difficult. While unintentional, living becomes more involved with an unforgiving attitude. We learn that seeking avoidance or vengeful ways to address relational issues adds another sticky layer of complication.

Do you have a difficult person in your life? Most of us do. Maybe it's a family member who is 180 degrees different in every way, or possibly a nosy co-worker or neighbor who causes ongoing grief. Spending a little personal time or working with them is never easy. Countless well-known books provide ample strategies, tips, and ideas for dealing with contrary people—yet the challenge persists.

The annoyance shoves its way into the forefront of everything we hold dear. It torments us 24/7 by its mere existence, screaming for immediate attention. Dealing with it may take more of our waking hours than we will ever have to devote. Dreams are devoured every sleepless night as it haunts our mind. The ordeal leaves us physically worn out and emotionally frazzled. We know dwelling on problems doesn't fix them. There is only more pain and less gain.

How do we handle challenging relationships? Different perspectives fuel varied approaches to addressing problems. Perhaps we consider our offender and designate them as the one responsible for dealing with the issue. After all, we didn't ask for this, did we? We only served as the hapless target receiving their ugliness. In this way, we may feel entitled to remove ourselves from the scene, rightfully claiming no fault in the matter.

This false sense of self-dispensed immunity provides us with unearned relief in the form of a welcomed assurance of no responsibility. We have summarily excused ourselves from any further involvement. We can walk away from it or place it on a high shelf, vowing never to look at it again. While this practice may seem reasonable, it is a common fallacy, because the glaring fact is a relationship with another remains hanging in the balance.

No matter how we view adversity or offense, there's no banishing it until it's addressed. Claiming it as someone else's mess does not clean it up. We're still involved in it, whether we want to be or not. Leaving it as unfinished business creates more pain and impedes our progress over the long run. Many mistakenly believe evidence can be buried, but there will be an eventual unearthing of it.

Wouldn't it be wonderful if there was an app for relieving uncomfortable situations? Imagine if repairing life's problems was as easy as checking off an item on our to-do list. The reason these strategies will never work is people are human beings, not human doings. Life brings us together with all kinds of people. Unlimited lessons on the importance of relationships result when we are willing to learn. Living life open to possibilities of developing and nurturing relationships with others has enormous benefits. We grow in maturity and better understanding of working with others. We discover blessings as our lives are enhanced by their presence. Our small world grows, extending far beyond our reach.

What the Bible Says about Relationships

It's tempting to pack an unwanted issue away for a while, but the Bible is clear about how we should conduct our interactions with others. Paul reminds us in Ephesians 4:2 to bear with one another in love. Jesus told His disciples, "This is my command: Love one another the way I loved you. This is the very best way to love" (John 15:12).

Lest we think that pesky person who always seems so needy or their endless time-intensive requests are over the top, we need to take stock of how God views each of us. If we're honest, we know He loves all of us, even those who create havoc or are hateful. We are commanded to love one another and not selectively.

. . .

The Bible tells us each person is unique, has remarkable gifts and value, and is called to live the life they've been given. Galatians 5:13-15 points out:

It is absolutely clear that God has called you to a free life. Just make sure that you don't use this freedom as an excuse to do whatever you want to do and destroy your freedom. Rather, use your freedom to serve one another in love; that's how freedom grows. For everything we know about God's Word is summed up in a single sentence: Love others as you love yourself. That's an act of true freedom. If you bite and ravage each other, watch out—in no time at all you will be annihilating each other, and where will your precious freedom be then?

So why should we waste our extraordinary gifts and promising life spent contrary to God's best for each of us?

Each Person Has Value, and We Can Learn from One Another

Every person has value in God's economy, even if we don't see it. This means that through our relationship with them, we can learn from them. They have different perspectives, ideas, and goals. This can be inspiring. Why should we shortchange ourselves by blocking opportunities to get to know them, to understand what their goals are, to see how we can help them? In the process, we will receive blessings back.

I'm reminded of the person everyone at the office passes by, never speaking as they hurry off to their next meeting or lunch. You may know that meek little worker who dedicates her day to every assigned task. Given only half a chance to talk about her interests and family could surprise a lot of people, revealing the beautiful person hiding behind the unassuming facade.

What about the person who misunderstood what you meant or

took something you said out of context? What if they grabbed a sound bite from you and ran with it? This calls for a clarifying moment through a heart-to-heart discussion. A conversation helps build relationships and spreads excellent ideas. Your next big idea may somehow be inspired in the process.

Together, We Can Make This World Better

Looking around and considering all the discord in the world, you might wonder about the real practicality of this approach. Wouldn't it be easier to keep interactions to a simple hello rather than getting into a detailed, full-blown discussion? It does seem like conversations are kept to a minimum with a growing list of topic taboos trending now.

God's instructions to us are to be mature. This means believers should be capable of having a civil conversation with anyone willing to join in.

Paul is clear about this in Ephesians 4:2-3:

In light of all this, here's what I want you to do. While I'm locked up here, a prisoner for the Master, I want you to get out there and walk—better yet, run!—on the road God called you to travel. I don't want any of you sitting around on your hands. I don't want anyone strolling off, down some path that goes nowhere. And mark that you do this with humility and discipline—not in fits and starts, but steadily, pouring yourselves out for each other in acts of love, alert at noticing differences and quick at mending fences.

As always, the way of the world sharply contrasts biblical instruction for believers, doesn't it? We know God is not behind the ways of the world, so why do we seek to live in that way? Why do we permit the prevailing thought-leaders to control our tongues, impact our personal relationships, and fundamentally impact our lives, when we feel afraid to talk about simple things with others? Relationships must take root somewhere. With time, attention, and nurturing they can grow.

Clearly, the world is not encouraging right relationships as flames of hate, violence, and conflict are fanned. Relationships cannot happen when people are alienated. Before we pass judgment on this unfortunate condition, we should pause to ask ourselves why we are allowing this to happen. We can take steps to fix a situation. We can begin in our own corner of the world by initiating honest, respectful, and loving personal conversations with others.

Imagine how incredible it would be to watch beautiful words spread like wildfire, burning in the hearts of all who hear. By our example, others are inspired and encouraged to do the same.

This is how God works in the world through His people:

So, chosen by God for this new life of love, dress in the wardrobe God picked out for you: compassion, kindness, humility, quiet strength, discipline. Be even-tempered, content with second place, quick to forgive an offense. Forgive as quickly and completely as the Master forgave you. And regardless of what else you put on, wear love. It's your basic, all-purpose garment. Never be without it. (Colossians 3:13-14)

Beloved, know this: God wants to bring us together in love. We are stronger and better together, held closely to Him. It is the world and Satan that want to divide and conquer.

Living God's way means we need to grant forgiveness and grace every chance we get. Unlike when we exercise, with mercy we can expect more gain and less pain for our effort.

When we move forward to restore a relationship, we will:

- Lessen our heavy burdens.
- Feel stronger, better, lighter, happier.
- Enjoy our life more, living with grace and peace.

UNDENIABLE TRUTH #2:
History isn't Written in Disappearing Ink

We often hear people sigh, shrugging off some ordeal, saying they will forgive and forget an incident. If you embrace this notion, how's it working for you? The truth is forgiving and forgetting is a timeworn notion misdirecting many for far too long. It is clear the offending incident happened, so attempting to live out this ideal is futile. Because the *wrong* is fact, it can never be erased from history. If it lies buried deep beneath piles of rubble, one day it may be unearthed. Turning our attention toward trying to forget about a matter impedes the essence of what forgiveness is about: loving from this painful place forward by forgiving. It's a bold step forward.

People tout "forgive and forget," maybe because this simply worded adage piles significant steps into a neat, manageable stack to ignore something painful. Doing this makes understanding forgiveness difficult and nearly impossible to achieve because the concept remains so immense, we can never get our arms around the idea to embrace it. True forgiveness doesn't mean you forget something hurtful. History can never be erased, nor can it be rewritten, but relationships can be restored at the broken places.

The act of forgiving doesn't condone or deny an action, nor ever promise to forget it. We can never transform wrong into appropriate behavior. We cannot accept it as permissible by explaining the reason it happened. But we can control how an unspeakable act impacts our life. By extending grace, any constricting hold over our lives can be released. Only then can we all move forward to resolution and life's joys that await discovery. This is the golden key to living free.

Remarkable bravery is required in forgiving. When the pain associated with a matter grows to an unbearable level, the need to resolve an issue becomes more significant than the distress of reliving it. Mustering great courage permits us to go into these dark places, root out the offending thing, ruthlessly tracing its origin. Admitting we made a misstep or confronting another involved in a painful situation compounds fear of taking steps toward resolution.

We like to avoid pain, don't we? Physical and emotional discomfort may be felt personally, or somehow manifested in cringe-worthy recognition of undeserved suffering. Most of us don't seek to relive the pain, and many don't want to inflict hurt on others.

Painful situations may grow to enormous proportions with little to no attention or care given. You may be shocked to discover a highly sensitive unmentionable incident super-sized itself into a painfully pulsating whopper, taking on the glowing neon appearance of a full-blown issue far too significant for anyone to ignore any longer.

Maybe the instigator tried to forget it or figured that somehow you (the injured) would eventually just get over it. In the perpetrator's mind, downplaying negative impact or denying personal involvement defuses the validity of a victim's claim. Rationalizing makes the incident easier for them to ignore, selfishly considering it as no big deal. This reframing of the situation as if it never happened spotlights the one who believes they have the most to lose—even in their attempt to appear otherwise—through aggressive defensive actions.

Isn't it interesting that quite often the one who would seem to have control over the photo-shopped optics and prepared statements has less power over their target? The foundation of their existence rests on the shifting sands of perception. Consider who digs the deepest moat around themselves, and you will know this is just a heavy-handed power play that does not hold up over the test of time. What matters most is what is. The truth can never be hidden forever.

Forgiveness and Reality are Based on What Is and Upon Truth

This is where we turn to the One who can help us see more

clearly and forgive more honestly. In this place we can leave our scheming mind and meddling, smart-mouth self outside the room. Jesus gently welcomes us with open arms as we come to Him in prayer, laying our hurting hearts, crushed spirits, and war-weary souls at His feet. We ask Him for help and forgiveness for our stubborn mind and contrary heart. He already knows all this, but He's patiently waiting to hear from us. We ask Him into this walled-off area, to help us sort through this disastrous mess.

Need proof? Here it is (Isaiah 41: 9-10):
    I pulled you in from all over the world, called you in from every dark corner of the earth, Telling you, "You're my servant, serving on my side. I've picked you. I haven't dropped you."
    Don't panic. I'm with you. There's no need to fear for I'm your God. I'll give you strength. I'll help you. I'll hold you steady, keep a firm grip on you.

It might take a lifetime to fully grasp this, but if you're in this place right now, dear reader, I pray you will stop reading and pray for God to remove the obstacles and strongholds now remaining in your way. It's not about you, me, or whatever we may believe should have been or never happened. It's all about getting real, seeing things as they are, knowing God has this, and He's right there with you to help you work out even the worst of things for His best and to bless you in ways you never imagined possible (Jeremiah 29:11).

    The truth is this: God is. He is all about truth. We can never go wrong when we bring our troubles to Him. He has promised to always be with us and He keeps His promises. He can help us face our daunting challenges, working through them to live the life He wants for each of us. He is love and truth. The truth will set you free (John 8:33c).

. . .

Revel in the Possibilities of Your Journey

Do you feel overwhelmed by a difficult situation you'd like to address? Maybe it seems massive or lies on a dark, frightening path. Undoubtedly, you wish you could avoid unpacking it. The thought of laying all the ugly pieces of it out in full view is repulsive. Still, a real need to address the matter nags, tugging at the corners of your mind. As the urgency grows intolerable, facing this matter can no longer be put off for the day you hoped would never come. Setting foot on an uncertain rocky trail can most assuredly scare the wits out of us, but our God stands by to help, offering us a lifeline. How do I know? I've had this experience too, friend.

God's assurance (Hebrews 13:6):

Since God assured us, "I'll never let you down, never walk off and leave you," we can boldly quote: God is there, ready to help; I'm fearless no matter what. Who or what can get to me?

This is a promise we can count on. I cannot imagine any greater assurance than knowing the Creator of the universe has our back in every aspect of our lives. He is far greater than our greatest fear or filthiest deed.

In the end, realizing no one can move past the trauma until a moment of orchestrated reconciliation occurs may cause a pivotal change in thinking about a troubling heart matter. A step taken toward absolution begins with what seems to be an agonizing process of releasing each from the tie that binds all involved in this issue. The binding is like a shared strand of invisible razor wire. Every step aches with deep pain. Removing it brings all closer to release and freedom from the self-imposed bondage unforgiving creates. It may be that to do otherwise will leave us trapped in the lonely prison of our mind, with an aching heart of what could have been and will never be otherwise.

Forgiveness is not reserved only for life's most malicious treacheries, unexpectedly inflicted upon the most innocent among us. Believers know compassion and mercy generously applied in those incidents is warranted. But extending grace and forgiveness is a daily decision for every moment we live. Some days invite us to experience a series of multiple opportunities to pardon others and to ask forgiveness ourselves, for matters great and small. In so doing, we free ourselves and others to move on through the day.

Jesus is all about unconditional love and forgiveness. This is grace. Grace is an extreme act of kindness. It is kneeling down in front of the other (literally or figuratively) to extend deeply desired absolution. It is generously extended in the spirit of honesty and authentic love. It is freely given—not always asked for, earned, expected, nor necessarily wanted.

The most significant example of grace is Jesus dying on the cross for our sins. In a pure stroke of who Jesus is, He asked God's forgiveness for all mankind, even as He was mocked (Luke 23:34-35):

Jesus prayed, "Father forgive them; they don't know what they're doing." Dividing up his clothes, they threw dice for them. The people stood there staring at Jesus, and the ringleaders made faces, taunting, "He saved others. Let's see him save himself! The Messiah of God — ha!"

By following Jesus' example, we can't go wrong. It isn't easy, but our human effort of getting it half right is always better than getting it all wrong by doing nothing at all. Even in cases where we did not bring the harm down upon ourselves, by not acting to restore a relationship or attempting amends, we are allowing the matter to stand as it is. We are endorsing it as the last word on the situation.

. . .

Feelings and Emotions Lead Us Down the Wrong Path

Do you know the difference between feelings and emotions? Do you ever consider whether you *feel* as if you could (or should) forgive someone? A common misconception confuses forgiveness as a feeling rather than the personal choice available to everyone at any time. Based on a rational decision, it is a step intentionally taken, whether we are ready or not. Either selection, forward or back, is a decision made, choosing to grant or withhold amnesty due. We may seize at once the opportunity as presented or let the cup pass. We may never *feel* ready to forgive and yet know deep down inside we must take a leap of faith and do it.

Emotions and feelings of pain are easily stirred from malicious incidents. Everything related to the despised situation is gathered into a feeling. I recently heard a doctor explain that feelings we perceive result from the body's chemical reaction to emotions experienced. Like the sick feeling we get thinking about something upsetting, or the lump in our throat making us feel immobilized.

Perhaps we rationalize this feeling and emotional packaging of an unforgiving attitude by thinking it provides a comfortable buffer, keeping us from any more hurt or greater anxiety if we were forced to relive that dread again. Still, traces of familiar sadness remain close, steeping every day in a bitter flavor of unresolved hurt. Through the test of time, it is clear a matter can never be resolved through any sort of self-medication or miles of separation.

Have you ever attempted to file an incident into the furthest recesses of your mind, believing you are then free to go on living your life? It's hard to take away what was done. It's equally pointless to continue stirring the boiling pot over a hot fire, especially after humble pie or crow has been eaten, or the rare delicacy of sweet words of forgiveness is served.

Sometimes pride (or unspeakable injury) influences our choices. The one who could extend grace remains deeply mired in the trauma that holds them back. It's important to know that forgiving another does not imply what was done is acceptable. The public is stunned when a murder victim's family speaks directly to the murderer in the courtroom. It is shocking to hear their Victim Impact Statement as they forgive his actions. The incident seems impossible to acquit. Somehow, it just doesn't feel right. How could they utter those words? We wonder if we ever could.

This is a prime example of misattributing the intentional act of absolution, which serves as an integral part of the healing process for those who have suffered loss. It is holding those involved accountable for the things they willfully engaged in by acknowledging it to them directly.

Once grace is extended, the next step is choosing to let go of the situation rather than hanging on to powerful emotions that prevent living life from commencing. This means cutting ties that bind all to the event. Releasing any sentimentality (including the desire to remain a victim) is essential. Doing this requires putting a lid on any simmering resentment and snuffing-out deep-seated emotions (grudges).

Sometimes, overwhelming issues cause resolving a matter to span weeks, years, or possibly a lifetime. With applied faith and resulting strength, it is possible to rebuild with the hope of living closer to our desired life. Beyond these necessary steps, establishing guidelines, boundaries, or rules may be required, especially in instances where personal safety is a concern. Seeking God's wisdom will help guide us through any daunting maze. Seeking a trusted and experienced godly counselor to further support our restoration efforts can help.

Sometimes, considering giving up on a particular relationship is justified when we haven't spoken with the person for so long, they've probably forgotten they ever knew us (not counting that one thing that happened the last time we did see them). If we are to follow the model (pattern) God has given us through His son Jesus Christ, walking away from a relationship is also rejecting His constant and everlasting love for us. When His love is so generously lavished on us as believers, we hold that love in our hearts. This allows us to weather any rough situation or relationship through Him.

UNDENIABLE TRUTH #3:

Forgiveness Doesn't Necessarily Create Reconciliation

The forgiven may never accept your grace, nor ever admit wrongdoing. Forgiving is a personal choice, mercifully offered out of true compassion by a heart that understands living a life of love (not revenge) is the opposite of doing nothing. It is lived out by decisively taking action to make things right.

Grace extended in truth and love sets us entirely free of living in the tangled mess of bondage called unforgiving. It gives up any rightful claim owed for mistreatment, with no punishment exacted for the harm or misfortune caused. Forgiveness is offered with an open hand while expecting nothing in return.

Why We Need Forgiveness

People are wired for connection with others. Examples of this basic need are played out all around us. Studies have shown babies thrive with their mother's touch. Much of society has participated in and observed the debilitating effects of isolation on individuals. An ongoing barrage of messages about relationships, their current state, and evolving status updates flash by in a continual life flow. Having the presence of others engaged in meaningful ways within our respective spheres of influence and lives is essential.

Relationship is a foundation for everything. It is the beginning and sometimes the end of living. It is the tie that binds us to all that is most important in our lives. Connectedness is what keeps us in touch with each other and provides much-needed support, serving as a safety net. Being part of something more significant beyond ourselves gives us a sense of purpose and place. Through attachment, a secure feeling of belonging somewhere emanates. It is reaching outward with intent to fill our inner selves, making each more complete, stronger, better.

God's love runs through us like a mighty river. It can easily overflow its banks within each of us at any time. We believe life is at its best when things are flowing smoothly. Because we are made in His image, we have his God-given traits to come together, to share and belong within the caring community. Isn't it a shame to see what was once a great river diminished to a mere trickle?

Just as our interconnectedness enhances our lives, our nature affects how we live, the things we do, our reactions and interactions with others. It is the underlying natural tendency that guides us, almost against our will or is even outside the boundaries of what we consider to be better judgment. This is where we can get into trouble. It is also the place where we may put our relationships most at risk. In this place, we're never quite sure where to safely pause, even a moment, and so we remain hopelessly nomadic. We grieve a loss as we wander in the wilderness, wondering how to put all the pieces back together.

The truth is things happen in life we will never understand. When the unimaginable intrudes into our lives, colliding with our hearts, we are left to choose how to handle it. Everyone has someone who needs grace or to be asked for forgiveness. No one is exempt. This is part of the human condition and is essential to grow relationships and live a dynamic life.

There are endless heartbreaking stories of mental, emotional, physical, and spiritual abuse. Sometimes, these are displayed publicly, while some occur in the pain-filled shadowy darkness saturated with silent cries. The air in that space forever hangs heavy with anguish and futility. There is no life found within those walls.

Maybe it started with a misstep no one could ever forgive. Or because the despised one is so different, no one knows what to do with them. Undeniable hatred spews out in fiery, flaming words. Perhaps it was nothing the object of vitriol did except being in the wrong place at precisely the right time. Somehow the maligned became involuntarily transformed into a convenient scapegoat for those who wish to insult, spread lies, gossip, or create false narratives through a simple wink and nod laced with innuendo, armed with burning intent to destroy.

For some, blaming, ridiculing, and venting on others is more comfortable than loving. Loving allows a vulnerable spot in the heart to remain exposed to hurt. Insecure people are unwilling to risk the hurt.

Unfortunately, they don't know they're limiting all possibility of profound joys and the full life they could otherwise enjoy. Perhaps they don't feel worthy or prefer to feed their comfort by pushing away from relationships, which might bring more personal pain. But maybe there would be more joys than pain. They don't know what they're missing. Their pain is great, but their true desire for resolution and joy plays a secondary role in life. They fear change in what they've grown accustomed to, and it is their world. They find comfort in the familiarity of their pain.

The cost of living this way is far higher than most imagine. Sporting an unforgiving attitude is personally wearing. It causes physical, emotional, mental, and relational problems, because we're choosing to do this on our own rather than turning to God, seeking His guidance and help. By going it alone, strictly under our own power (by not resting in Him), we cannot continue for long without showing signs of wear.

Eventually, we may grow weary by unresolved issues weighing us down. We stay busy punching at shadows, trying to protect ourselves. All attempts to fend off more pain are futile because the pain already surrounds us in our prison. Because we are not living in faith this way, an unforgiving spirit also hurts us spiritually. It drives a wedge between God and us, further grieving the Holy Spirit (Galatians 2:20).

Think for a moment of the most successful people you know or have observed. Even while these individuals seem to have everything going for them, they highly prize their relationship with others. Just like us, their relationships offer ample opportunities to forgive.

Those we witness living remarkable lives, their success recognizable through incredible achievements, frequently attain awe-inspiring goals and live their dream. They learned long ago how to repair, restore, and nurture relationships with others in a caring way.

These successful people didn't get to their level of prosperity or incredible level of success on their own, but by actively building teams, partners, and support systems. They created extensive networks. To be effective, they know that an expanding sphere of influence is essential, looking always to include more rather than to exclude or snub selectively. They not only hold these relationships in high regard, they actively seek to encourage their friends, colleagues, and family to do their best.

Because they believe there are enough good things for everyone, they don't feel threatened nor fear competition. Through their advanced relational skills, realizing the importance of stable relationships with others, these remarkable people (who genuinely care about others) have become inspiring success stories in all fields.

If nothing else, recognizing this fact should prompt each of us to pull a page from their playbook and move forward to live our own inspired lives. Why would we want to hold ourselves back from what could be possible? Don't settle for less. Seek God's best through a deeper connection with Him and in true relationship with others.

The heart provides fertile ground for the seeds of change in life. Through a rich, nurturing environment, good things develop from scattering a few pure seeds. For this to happen, our heart must be open to accept the possibilities, beyond what we know (or believe) to become our reality. Prayer is the way to begin tilling that soil. Ask God to open your heart for things He wants for you. Pray for Him to make you aware of things you might be missing and for His guidance in moving ahead. Listen. Watch for His answer. There is power (and an answer) in waiting on Him (Romans 12:11-12).

Incredible freedom will fill our lives once we can accept as blessing whatever comes our way. On this segment of our journey, letting go of the white-knuckled grasp of things proven to not work, is freeing.

It's plain to see our control issues serve as hindrances to realizing our heart's desire. God can use this for good. The result comes as opportunities beyond our wildest imagination. In the process we grow closer to Him, gaining clarity about what is right and true. If this is left unchecked, we can do a real number on ourselves, because we inherently have enough evil tendencies in our heart to further ensnare ourselves or cause yet another self-inflicted wound (Jeremiah 17:9). We all need to forgive because it is a soothing salve for hatred and anger.

Forgiving is Not Easy, But It Is Always Right

Christians are called to follow a higher standard. This requires us to step up. We are to take our stand based on God's directives and His expectations for us. Doing the hard things in life usually involves doing the right things. Because taking action is difficult, people will try to avoid it at all costs. When they attempt it, they tend to meander around the truth rather than dealing more directly with the problem.

Avoid oversimplification of a matter. Downplaying something makes it seem like it isn't worth all the bother and attention. This gives the false impression it's possibly not as important as everyone knows it really is. We wouldn't be having a conversation about it if it were not at all concerning.

Sin is sin in God's eyes. His view sharply contrasts man's perspective of what comprises sin as we daily sweep great offenses and grievances under the rug. Call things for what they are. Sin is, in essence, doing all manner of stupid things that are wrong in God's eyes. Sin causes great pain and will never make sense to us.

Stupid things [sin] require forgiveness. Forgive the stupid thing done or ask to be forgiven for the foolish thing you did. Crazy things happen. We're all human beings and suffer bouts of *stupid*. This is a specialty of our humanness, even for those who may not ever wish to admit it. We all share this trait.

It's important to keep in mind that as we work toward forgiveness, no one is superior to another. We are always on the same level, all of us loved equally by God.

The truth is we can forgive—and must. How is this possible? We are assured of being wired for love. Loving others and living a life of forgiveness is possible. Here's how (1 John 4:19): "We, though, are going to love—love and be loved. First, we were loved, now we love. He loved us first."

Forgiving in Real Life: Apply the Principles and Live these Truths by Prayerful Preparation

Prepare your heart. Bravely face situations and challenging relationships with an open heart to accept possibilities beyond what is known or imagined. They may become a new and better reality.

Scripture instructs us to let go of past offenses, things that bind us to our torment, to release negative thoughts and dispense with self-disparaging views that serve to hold us back from God's best. We cannot control what happens to us, but in Christ, we can control how we handle unexpected life challenges (Ephesians 3:14-19).

Action steps

Pray, asking God to open your heart to things He wants for you.

Pray for Him to make you aware of what you're missing.

Ask for His guidance in moving ahead.

Listen. Watch for His answer. There is power and an answer in your waiting on Him. Be ready.

THREE
FORGIVING ME

Forgiving Me is the Problem

While writing this book, I've spoken with many people who freely opened their hearts to me on the spot, telling me of their forgiveness challenges. Some shared their secret inability to forgive themselves over unnamed matters in their lives. They do believe they're able to forgive others (some, at least in part) but never themselves.

Perhaps they (humanly) expected better of themselves, and denying absolution is their way of self-punishment. This practice is as if they are placing *self* into a perpetual time-out corner. Maybe they continue to mourn the loss of a person or deeply regret the experience they failed to embrace, now forever lost. Whatever their intention, obviously this strategy didn't help loosen the grip of sadness and pain caused by their misstep or circumstances. They continue to hold themselves hanging in limbo, in a never-ending cycle of suffering.

I'm sure I could name all manner of *reasons* for this, because man's rationale for behavior is as diverse as individual personalities that have roamed the earth since time began. While endless justifications abound, not one of them is well-founded. All of the explanations serve only to capture and hold anyone willing to fall into the trap to remain imprisoned for as long as they allow. Even when an incident occurs or an issue exists, Christ followers never have the privilege to withhold forgiveness. Therefore, we must also forgive ourselves.

Our unconfessed (admitted) sin leads to instability in life. It affects us mentally, physically, and wears us down. God does forgive and offers His gift of salvation to all. Through our own free will, we may accept it. When we do receive His grace, we become His followers. As believers, we embrace His precepts to love and forgive, following His example. This follows God's commands to us throughout the Bible, but don't take my word for it.

Here's what Paul wrote about this (Ephesians 1:3-10):

How blessed is God! And what a blessing he is! He's the Father of our Master, Jesus Christ, and takes us to the high places of blessing in him. Long before he laid down earth's foundations, he had us in mind, had settled on us as the focus of his love, to be made whole and holy by his love. Long, long ago he decided to adopt us into his family through Jesus Christ. (What pleasure he took in planning this!) He wanted us to enter into the celebration of his lavish gift-giving by the hand of his beloved Son.

Because of the sacrifice of the Messiah, his blood poured out on the altar of the Cross, we're a free people—free of penalties and punishments chalked up by all our misdeeds. And not just barely free, either. *Abundantly* free! He thought of everything, provided for everything we could possibly need, letting us in on the plans he took such delight in making. He set it all out before us in Christ, a long-range plan in which everything would be brought together and summed up in him, everything in deepest heaven, everything on planet earth.

. . .

Let's take a closer look at what this Scripture says:
- Our heavenly Father has incredibly blessed each of us with every spiritual blessing available in heaven, through His Son Jesus Christ! (verse 3)
- Even before He created the heavens and earth, He had a plan for all; we were part of it, chosen as His to be holy and blameless in His love. (verse 4)
- His plan included our salvation (forgiveness) through Jesus Christ; we are adopted sons and daughters into His family. (verse 5)
- God's heartfelt desire is for us to join in great celebration, praising and thanking Him for His gracious grace He poured out abundantly upon us. (verse 6)

Because the Bible is God's message to all of us, we can read it with understanding that it gives assurance and needed instruction. Through careful study and contemplation of His Word, we gain understanding and guidance in applying His principles in our lives.

If we, as believers, can accept the facts as laid out in Ephesians 1:3-6, then we must also fully embrace what the rest of this passage tells us (verses 7-10):
- Through Jesus' death, we receive forgiveness of sin and salvation, wiping our life's slate clean to live forgiven and free of all of our transgressions. (verse 7)
- In our minds we may think we're forgiven of a certain misdeed, but God's grace is lavished over everything we've done or ever will do. (verse 8)
- In His infinite wisdom, He knew every twist and turn in our future, lovingly making provision for them, already knowing all about us and our needs. (verse 9)
- Everything in our life begins and ends in Him, extending to the ends of the earth, resounding throughout heaven. It is *for* us, but not all *about* us. (verse 10)

The Bottom Line

We are His. He has blessed us well beyond our understanding. His love wraps us completely in forgiveness through our salvation granted to us with Jesus' ultimate sacrifice. God is not selective in what He will forgive. All our misdeeds are forgiven. If we are God's children, we must accept His entire gift, or we will surely miss out on His intended blessing.

This passage of Scripture clearly presents the undeniable gifts of God's forgiveness, grace, and love that have generously been lavished upon all of us as His children. To refuse the gifts as ours, instead of embracing His forgiveness, is to deny the sovereignty of God. Quite simply, it is putting *self* ahead of Him and our relationship with Him —our own Father. In doing so, we allow whatever we think, feel, and decide for ourselves to rule over our lives, instead of handing over the rein to Him. He is maker of heaven and earth, greater than all of us.

But It Began with Me

Have you ever felt hopelessly unforgivable? Maybe this pervasive feeling is because of something you said or did. Maybe you're the victim of circumstances because of the way something happened. No human has ever lived without making a mistake. Each of us has to consider how our mistakes impact our relationships. What begins with us is to acknowledge how we view our role in the shameful incident and evaluate where we stand with God on it. We may feel it began with us, but ultimately it ends with Him and His Word.

It's difficult to admit a wrongdoing, recognize our own shortcomings, unintentional errors, and blunders, or admit our mistreatment of another. We think we already know all our imperfections. Steeped in pride, we work hard to hide them from the discriminating public eye. We rationalize that telling all through admission is like putting everything out there for the world to see.

Even if we personally initiated a wrongful deed or received an affront and reacted badly to it, none of it truly begins with self. Our everything begins with God. How we live daily is reflective of our relationship with Him. How we address life challenges, deal with our perplexing problems, treat others, and respond to everything is influenced by how we have embraced His gift. It is relative to the degree we have Him personally involved in our life.

All problems punctuating life give God opportunity to bring us back to Him. His holding us closer allows us to trust Him more. While it's difficult to admit our offense, when we can't find the words to own it, the deep sting of regret lingers.

We may mistakenly believe it is possible for us to fix our brokenness all by ourselves. No matter how strong or able we're convinced we are, we cannot fix any problem nor exist entirely on our own. For the same reason, we cannot forgive ourselves alone.

Believers understand that God wants to be involved in every aspect of our lives—including restoring the broken places. Forgiving ourselves is not a DIY procedure. God already provided for us, well ahead of our recognized need. The sure way is willingly opening our hearts and trusting Him to help us through. Already forgiven and free, we must fully accept His gift and live the life He wants for us, wrapped in His love, experiencing joy and peace at last.

In our uncertain world, there are two inescapable facts we can count on:
- We (will) do stupid things [sin].
- He can, will, does, and has forgiven us.

These demonstrable truths are based on the understanding that God is almighty, and we are human. He can make things right, but we need to include Him in the process and accept His grace. In order to do this as His followers, we must take Him at His Word. We must fully believe that what He says also applies to us, not just those with whom we share relational challenges. We are never exempt. Feeding the mindset that we are unworthy of His grace (or to receive anyone's forgiveness) in any matter holds us in a place we'd always rather escape. This is the place He will always relentlessly pursue us in His desire to free us.

Here is a clear sign of putting self before all, even setting up elaborate barriers to get in our own way of restoration. If after reading Ephesians 1:3-10, we're still saying to ourselves, "Yes, but ..." In other words, we're openly accepting God's grace, but inwardly we're not acting on it in love.

Since this heart condition is reflected in our lives for all to see, we are only fooling ourselves. We may willingly extend forgiveness freely to all as seemingly the kindest person. Meanwhile, we remain locked up in our own shackles by not forgiving ourselves. We are eternally held captive in our own personal prison of perpetual punishment. Sentenced to be kept here indefinitely under the guise of forcing ourselves to maintain *our* standards. We remain hidden away down the dark, dank hall of guilt.

If this is you—and you already threw away the keys to your prison cell and handcuffs—take heart. You can be freed. Nothing can separate you from Him. Believing everything begins (and ultimately ends) with *me* is a huge self-created obstacle between God and us. He is the Alpha and Omega. We are His beloved.

Let your heart hear Paul's prayer for the Colossians, which is also a prayer for us (Colossians 1:11-14):

Be assured that from the first day we heard of you, we haven't stopped praying for you, asking God to give you wise minds and spirits attuned to his will, and so acquire a thorough understanding of the ways in which God works. We pray that you'll live well for the Master, making him proud of you as you work hard in his orchard. As you learn more and more how God works, you will learn how to do *your* work. We pray that you'll have the strength to stick it out over the long haul—not the grim strength of gritting your teeth but the glory-strength God gives. It is strength that endures the unendurable and spills over into joy, thanking the Father who makes us strong enough to take part in everything bright and beautiful that he has for us.

God rescued us from dead-end alleys and dark dungeons. He's set us up in the kingdom of the Son he loves so much, the Son who got us out of the pit we were in, got rid of the sins we were doomed to keep repeating.

God, Jesus, and the Holy Spirit existed before the earth was created. God had a heartfelt desire and a grand plan to create heaven and earth, and we were a major part of His holy plan. He provided all we needed to live life here, equipping us with an incredible spirit that is connected to Him. His Word gives us understanding of His ways and instructions on how we should live a great life in Him. He knew it wouldn't be easy for us in this life, but He never left us to our own devices and abilities to deal with our challenges alone. He is faithful through His provision and in keeping His promises.

Staying near to Him helps us through difficult, daunting times. How remarkable when we discover the ultimate joy as an unthinkable thing turns into an unbelievable blessing. Our prayers and groans to Him transform into praise and thanks as we eventually gain a glimpse of the amazing grace He has abundantly poured down upon us. Humbled by His immense love, we see how He brought us through to the other side because we faithfully followed step-by-step with a willing heart to keep Him in our lives and eyes wanting to see His beauty, leaving all else behind.

Looking for Forgiveness in All the Wrong Places

We can easily look for forgiveness in wrong places, but it leads us away from restoration, taking us where we don't need to be. It always keeps us from living the kind of life we desire most. We may have difficulty forgiving ourselves, but we know God never runs out of grace and forgiveness for us.

Here are some everyday examples:
- **Deception:** When asked how we are, we readily reply "fine," putting on a performance to fool others or deny personal issues.
- **Distraction:** When we become busy with so many things, we literally have no time to think, so we simply divert our focus away from a problem.
- **Despair:** Things become confusing as reality is distorted, coupled with discouragement caused by believing the world's lies.

Simple truths are tucked away awaiting our discovery throughout the Scriptures. Sometimes, what appears to be an uncomplicated concept turns out to be much more difficult for us to do than we ever thought possible. In those moments when we lack clarity, realizing we are standing in our own way to fully accept God's blessings, is a step in the right direction toward making a necessary repair in our relationship with Him.

Our true acceptance of all He has for us begins with our own dying to self by putting Him first. This means more of our Father in our lives and much less of self. We do this by praising Him, thanking Him, and turning it all over to Him. We look for where He leads us. He is able, ready, and waiting.

This is the way God works. His ways are opposite to man's ways:
- Since we are here on earth for God's pleasure, we are His creation and are meant to fellowship with Him.
- Pointing others to Him, our me-centric living obscures the view of Him through us.
- Not fulfilling His purpose, we miss out on His blessings.

. . .

To find our life with Him, we need to lose our life—all of it. Not forgiving ourselves colors our world with a broad, messy brush of uncertainty. True joy is lacking. We may be known to have quite the sense of humor, but what type of humor is it? Is it a monologue of self-effacing commentary, slicing close to the bone? Is it cutting—too quick to be truly thoughtful? Is it never quite witty enough to build a bridge for closer relationships, repelling others by a sarcastic, uncaring nature?

It's possible to fool ourselves by thinking this works for us. Sometimes that humorous side turns out to be a wax mask that will melt on the spot when things begin heating up.

Our attitudes about forgiveness, our willingness to admit mistakes, and how we ask for and grant grace presents another face to those who watch—perhaps family and children. Steeped in these attitudes, established traditions and practices develop. What is reaped by the seeds sown results in a crop that is tilled for generations from now. How do you want to be remembered? Old wounds effectively keep families apart yet forever linked in painful memories, never freed and afraid to try.

Since all of this is so uncomfortable, why do we permit ourselves to remain locked up in the pain we've caused? Could it be we believe we deserve to relive the horror by continually punishing ourselves the best way we can every day? The problem is, as with any unforgiving spirit, it doesn't work. Man's idea of punishment is different. God's treatment of our wrongs is profound and expansive (Luke 23:41).

Living Forward in Love and with Forgiveness

Of course, we are given free will to accept Jesus' invitation, to fully embrace God's grace and decide how we will live. In so choosing, we will receive the consequences of our decision. What will your choice be? This I know: when we change our mindset by focusing our lives entirely on Jesus, following Him wholeheartedly, astonishing things with remarkable long-lasting effects occur.

God wants to prosper us and has generously provided everything we need. Why would we choose a more difficult, less fulfilling life? To live otherwise is not fully living in Him. It's living as our old self, not our new self in Christ. Focus not on when that thing happened, or what it was, but on Him. Keep your eyes on Jesus.

When Jesus came to earth, showed us how to live, then died on the cross for our sins, everything changed. Here's how (2 Corinthians 5:17-20):

Because of this decision we don't evaluate people by what they have or how they look. We looked at the Messiah that way once and got it all wrong, as you know. We certainly don't look at him that way anymore. Now we look inside, and what we see is that anyone united with the Messiah gets a fresh start, is created new. The old life is gone; a new life burgeons! Look at it! All this comes from the God who settled the relationship between us and him, and then called us to settle our relationships with each other. God put the world square with himself through the Messiah, giving the world a fresh start by offering forgiveness of sins. God has given us the task of telling everyone what he is doing. We're Christ's representatives. God uses us to persuade men and women to drop their differences and enter into God's work of making things right between them. We're speaking for Christ himself now: Become friends with God; he's already a friend with you.

We must allow ourselves to be loved—by God and by others. We must care enough ...

If you are allowing yourself to remain imprisoned in your unforgiving mindset, this is your own choosing. Admitting grievous error may be difficult, but not allowing yourself to own it keeps you from God's best and living closer to Him.

Dwelling on not forgiving yourself holds you back. Decide to let go of it. This is not your burden to bear alone—or forever. Jesus is the key to your freedom. All you have to do is call on Him. He's always waiting to hear from you. Don't deny yourself God's incredible blessings awaiting you, nor the most powerful friendship you will ever have.

Scripture assures us of this (Romans 6:6-11):

Could it be any clearer? Our old way of life was nailed to the cross with Christ, a decisive end to that sin-miserable life—no longer at sin's every beck and call! What we believe is this: If we get included in Christ's sin-conquering death, we also get included in his life-saving resurrection. We know that when Jesus was raised from the dead it was a signal of the end of death-as-the-end. Never again will death have the last word. When Jesus died, he took sin down with him, but alive he brings God down to us. From now on, think of it this way: Sin speaks a dead language that means nothing to you; God speaks your mother tongue, and you hang on every word. You are dead to sin and alive to God. That's what Jesus did.

This is a new day.

When we finally come to the end of ourselves, we will find God. Keeping our eyes on Jesus brings us through. Looking to Him, we cannot fail. We are loved, refined by the fire, and rescued by our Lord and Savior Jesus Christ. Our future is secure through Him (1 Peter 1:6-7).

Miracles arise from the ashes of destruction. Remarkable transformations reflect His unfailing love, along with His endless grace, peace, and incomparable power. In our times of trials, and when we finally seek Him, we learn to trust fully in God for His way and His truth as we follow His light.

Forgiving in Real Life: Apply the Principles and Live these Truths by Personal Reflection

Take a close look at how you view forgiveness. Do you find it easier to extend grace to others and almost never forgive yourself? Are there occasions when you can more easily forgive yourself?

Consider what the parameters of your preferences are for forgiving yourself. Maybe you've never considered how you continue to torture yourself because "you know better" and hold yourself to a higher standard. Do you not think God already knows?

Action step

He's ready to meet you there. Talk to Him about this. This is a divine appointment not to be missed—go!

FOUR
FORGIVING THEM

The Case for Forgiveness

The case for forgiveness is clearly laid out for all to see in the powerful words of 1 John 4:7-21. This passage answers questions many ask in seeking definitive proof about this subject and receiving needed clarity on what love is, as a Christian. There is much to glean from these words, so let's break them down verse-by-verse.

Love Is a Gift from God (verse 7)

Why we love, where love comes from, and how it is an inherently human trait—as a gift from God—is clearly attributed. John tells us we are capable of loving because love is from God. As believers, we are born of God. Everyone who loves has been born of God and knows Him. We're hardwired for this through our own unbreakable connection with Him:

My beloved friends, let us continue to love each other since love comes from God. Everyone who loves is born of God and experiences a relationship with God.

. . .

How Love Exists in the First Place (verse 9)

God's love was revealed to us when He sent His Son Jesus into the world for our salvation. Through His life and crucifixion, He illustrated what living a life of true love looks like:

This is how God showed his love for us: God sent his only Son into the world so we might live through him.

What Love Consists Of (verse 10)

It wasn't that we loved God, but rather He first loved us so much that He sacrificed His one and only Son to atone for our sins, giving anyone who will believe and accept His gracious invitation to have eternal life with Him:

This is the kind of love we are talking about—not that we once upon a time loved God, but that he loved us and sent his Son as a sacrifice to clear away our sins and the damage they've done to our relationship with God.

How We Are to Love (verse 11)

Because God loves each of us so much, we are expected to love others by following His example. The ultimate sacrifice came when His Son died to pay our sins ahead for us. Surely, most of us would never make such a significant sacrifice, even while forgiving another may seem to be a daunting impossibility to us:

My dear, dear friends, if God loved us like this, we certainly ought to love each other.

How We Can Love Beyond the Hurt (verse 13)

Sometimes we're amazed when we understand we can still love someone who needs our forgiveness, possibly a person we've already forgiven, or who has done terrible things. Here's how:

This is how we know we're living steadily and deeply in him, and he in us: He's given us life from his life, from his very own Spirit.

Years ago, I was surprised when my youngest son told me he observed I could not hate. Honestly, I'd never thought about it. I guess I'd never realized this because it is my way of life, living in Him. Some may wonder if it's possible. It is.

Many times I have been swept away with waves of extreme gratefulness (and a lot of tears) when I think of how I have been incredibly blessed. I believe we can spend our lives buried in deep sadness and remain eternally wounded for what we never had or maybe had for a short time and lost. Or we can choose to accept beautiful blessings and God's best in our lives.

Why True Believers Cannot Hate and the Process of Love (verses 19-20)

It's about Him more than it is about us, because there will be times when we don't feel inclined to be caring or show love to another but should:

We, though, are going to love—love and be loved. First, we were loved, now we love. He loved us first. If anyone boasts, "I love God," and goes right on hating His brother or sister, thinking nothing of it, he is a liar. If he won't love the person he can see, how can he love the God he can't see?

I remember hearing *love* defined as a process of give and take between amiable parties. Based on this idea, reciprocity is the defining essence of a real relationship. While I'm not convinced this is always the basis of a mutual affinity-type arrangement, this passage clearly lays out how this works in God's realm, and it makes sense. Loving others glorifies Him. It's not about setting up elaborate networks of people to care for and in turn be cared for by them in equal measure.

. . .

Jesus' Command (verse 21)

Sometimes we think we have a choice, or maybe choose to love selectively. Truthfully, based on this Scripture, loving and forgiving are not choices. No matter how difficult we think (or feel) it is, it can be done:

The undeniable command we have from Christ is blunt: Loving God includes loving people. You've got to love both.

There are always people in our lives who are infinitely easier to love. Some seem impossibly difficult to remain in a loving relationship with. This Scripture reminds us we are called to a higher standard in our way of living life as Christians. Negligence of personal responsibility and reckless disregard for truth is always unacceptable.

The Definitive: Why, Where, How, What, and When of Loving and Forgiving Explained

Using these passages as a framework for understanding, we can see that the answer to the big question of *why* we are to forgive [God is love] encloses the first and last statements of this argument, in this case for forgiveness. This is fitting because He is the beginning and end of all things. He is the Alpha and Omega of everything (Revelation 1:8, 22:13).

It is because of Him (and through Him) we are loved, do love, and are capable of loving others. It is because of our love of Him, we must love others. Loving others in this way glorifies God, and that pleases Him. Loving others means always extending grace to them whenever necessary.

Jesus' clear command is to love and be loved. Our ability to genuinely love God is only possible when we love (not hate) all people unequivocally, with no exceptions or based on our personal preferences. We are all part of God's family, so this should not come as a surprise to anyone. However, based on the heated tenor of conversations and how relationships have been regarded, especially in recent years, there are some who have forgotten or not recognized this.

This is how we love God: by unconditionally loving all and freely forgiving. If we say we're followers of Christ and love God as the Scriptures state, it's clear we are to love others and never withhold grace. Love and forgiveness go with the territory of being a Christian. So why do we convince ourselves otherwise? Even as mature Christians, a number of factors can come into play, influencing our lives and choices.

The World's Lies Captivate

Worldly ways and beliefs compete for everyone's attention. Through the power of peer pressure and new ideas or practices (regardless of how unbecoming or inappropriate), these may be swept up and carried far by a tidal wave of popular approval.

Widely recognized and encouraged by society, lives are greatly influenced in countless ways by it daily. As a result, relationships are forever impacted. The resulting impression left on society may be positive or create deep divides and further relational erosion. Here are some examples of how this phenomenon occurs.

Words of Love Can Unintentionally Become Inflammatory

Try as we may to steer clear of elements deemed as not Christlike, the world still has an insidious way of infiltrating our everyday life. Even when we attempt to avoid the bulk of filth flowing in with each tide, a dingy residual sometimes remains, lining the shoreline of life.

It may begin by simply making an innocent statement. Because they listened from a different perspective, someone overreacts, thinking you meant something completely different from your intent or your message. Or perhaps they have strong convictions and refuse to accept what you say as truth or see any value in it. Maybe they became offended because you mentioned something outside certain parameters they will never discuss or are unwilling to converse with those they are sure think radically different (or wrong) compared to their understanding.

Code words, politically charged words, misused words, and words with multiple meanings to different people easily fan the flames of discord, creating misunderstanding and hardship in relationships today. Or—when cooler heads with listening hearts prevail—these moments can offer a time of clarification and meaningful dialogue.

In those sweet times of fellowship, lasting relationships are strengthened, and true community may be built (Ephesians 4:15).

The Fallacy of Inclusiveness

The respecter of all ways respects none because eventually establishing standards and choosing a personal tradition of belief to follow becomes necessary. Honoring all ways and beliefs as a sacred way is the intentional act of holding no beliefs at all. If all are worthy of honor, then, in reality, none are. They are all lumped into the same jumbled pile.

This approach is different than recognizing that others have differing opinions, varying sets of beliefs, and respecting their inalienable right to do so, while not upholding or supporting their personal beliefs (of which we are not a part). In a world filled with constant foundational change and continually evolving philosophies, it's no wonder people become confused. What *was* yesterday is no longer today. Who knows what tomorrow will bring? Answer: God does (Matthew 24:36).

We must step out in faith and live courageously without needing others to come to our defense. Our God is the same today as He has been throughout time. He will be the same tomorrow. On this we can rest. He has withstood the test of time and is faithful.

In relationships, Jesus is inclusive. During His time on earth, He fellowshipped with people from all walks of life. His teaching touched the hearts of all people who heard Him, even those who chose not to believe Him. His invitation to follow Him, to believe and come and live with Him in heaven forever is freely offered to all people who are willing to take the leap of faith and accept His loving offer to leave their ways and receive God's forgiveness (Ephesians 4:25).

Who's Running Our Life?

Each of us has been given the gift of life. It is ours to live as we choose. While here on earth, we can freely use the gifts we've been blessed with to make this a better place as we serve our Lord and Savior.

Living mindfully, keeping our purpose in plain view, helps guide our steps. Frequent unanticipated interruptions in our journey and unnecessary incidents that threaten to interfere with and impede our endeavors are merely an inevitable fact of earthly existence.

In chaotic times, unusual opportunities to diverge into strange new territory can mispresent themselves as seemingly attractive possibilities. In that moment, this new thing seems right—but is it?

Here are some examples and guiding strategies:
- We suddenly find ourselves thrust into a situation that seems to be a natural lead-in to embrace beliefs and practices not part of the Christian tradition, but rather as dictated by worldly views. They seem harmless enough, and lots of people are participating. Would this be wrong to do?
- Our view on a personal matter is negatively impacting a family relationship. It colors our perspective, hurts our heart, and causes difficult communication with them. We believe this is not what God

had in mind for His children, and it's wrong. We want to put this matter to rest, but how? Is it right or wrong?

• A huge life decision must be made. We're not provided with a lot of options, only limited information. The choice is either yes or no. What to do?

Many of the world's lies are the fertile seeds of adversity that easily sprout arguments. It's interesting that nurtured under the right conditions, these seeds can also propagate restoration and grow relationships. It all depends upon how we choose to live our lives and tend to the seeds we sow. The lens with which we view events, along with words and actions, is colored by the life we're living.

We must always be cautious about power given to others over our lives. Just because someone says (or we think) something is a certain way doesn't make it so. Only God can speak things into existence (Genesis 1:3-31). Letting others influence us regarding what is right and true is also dangerous. This is when digging into God's Word can help navigate through challenging and confusing times.

Mixed Messages

An example of mixed messages that confuse real life issues centers around when touching others is appropriate or inappropriate. Much of the public seems to agree that to touch another without consent is inappropriate. This includes a perpetrator taking advantage of a situation if an individual is somehow compromised and cannot defend themselves, or a person of authority uses their status to molest a subordinate. In both cases, the villain believes no one will ever know, because the injured is not in a position to report the incident, nor likely to be believed if they do.

Sadly, public tolerance of unwanted touching sometimes becomes permissive, depending upon *who* it is, especially if by a kindly older person whom they know means no harm. The fact remains that unwanted touching happened to another but is allowed to pass through the filter of public scrutiny at the victim's expense. This is an example of how, if we let public thought direct our lives, we will never live as God intends. Instead, we will live in a way that embraces the world's ways (Proverbs 4).

Letting emotions rule life is to ignore God's higher standards by going our own way, disregarding Christian principles for exceptional living. It might seem logical or even natural to go with our gut feeling in addressing a problem.

Emotions start in the brain, then create a response within our bodies. This physiological effect may occur due to the natural release of chemicals or hormones. Sometimes a signal is sent to another part of the body such as the heart. How we *feel* may also be influenced by other contributing physical factors impacting the brain's mood-regulation ability. Separating our actions from these natural physical reactions that create perceived *feelings* keep the impact of personal emotions in check.

The importance of *heart* is stressed in different situations but should never be applied for discernment on matters from that human perspective. Heart represents love, passion, and our best of intentions as defined by the world. At its core it is a spiritual condition as natural as breathing for believers: living in God's truth and following Jesus' lead in love, as God intended. It's part of being one of God's children. When we act, we are given the capability of showing love, coming from a place of truth, and praising God in the process. What flows in love from the believer's heart is not from us; it's a blessing from God, and all praise goes back to Him.

Look Before You Leap

Are you in a quandary, trying to decide what to do now? The answer may surprise you, but ... look it up in the Bible. Study all around the Word, seeking greater understanding. Don't be afraid to do this but do be fully prepared to be surprised.

There have been many times when I have gone deep-diving into Scripture for answers only to emerge refreshed, amazed, and better informed. Even what we believe to be right and true, including ideas and practices we may have grown up with (or thought we remembered), may have changed within us incrementally over the years.

The question to ask is are these perspectives in line with biblical principles? Is this as God intended? The way to know for sure is to dig deep into God's infallible, unchanging Word.

It's always good to get a spiritual check-up. When special questions or pressing issues arise, it's essential. Jesus is our plumb-line measure to see if our lives are right and true. The answer is always found in the Bible.

Taking biblical principles or Scripture and interpreting them to fit a narrative, to support or promote our own idea or a personal preference, is never appropriate. It is not up to us (or the world) to rewrite, dilute, or modify God's love letter to us. It's always well worth the time spent in personal Bible study. Ultimately, the results are long-lasting by gaining a deeper understanding. Through study and reflection, we benefit from new insights that can be applied to improve our lives and relationships. It's up to us to find out what the Bible instructs us to do and then reshape our lives to follow Jesus (Matthew 7:7).

Note: If you have children, you alone are responsible for teaching them these basic principles. If you don't, they risk being ensnared by the world's lies. Even with your best prayerful instruction to them, they may be fooled by an exaggeration or misrepresentation, possibly believing a falsehood for a while. Take heart and comfort in remembering what Scripture says about our children's future when they are brought up with biblical standards and principles (Proverbs 22:6).

Walking in Forgiveness

One of the most memorable and touching Bible stories that exemplifies the principal of forgiveness is that of Joseph, his brothers, and the coat of many colors (Genesis 37-50). Joseph was the youngest son of Jacob, who was the son of Isaac and Rebekah, and Esau's twin brother. God changed Jacob's name to Israel. His twelve sons became the heads of the twelve tribes of Israel. Their descendants became known as the children of Israel.

Joseph was the youngest in the family. Scripture tells us he was Jacob's favorite. Jacob made Joseph an elaborate coat, which caused his brothers to be jealous. Joseph had two prophetic dreams and told them to his brothers and father. The interpretation of them implied Joseph would reign over his family one day. This caused the brothers to hate him even more. They began to plot his demise.

Honoring his father's request to go check on his brothers and the flock they were pasturing, Joseph left the valley of Hebron in search of them. Filled with vengeance for their little brother, when Joseph reached the group, they stripped him of his multicolored coat and threw him in a cistern. After a meal, a caravan of Ishmaelites from Gilead approached. Judah suggested it would be more profitable if they sold Joseph into slavery instead of killing him. So, his brothers sold Joseph to the Midianite merchants for twenty shekels of silver. The brothers fabricated a story about their brother's untimely end. They dipped his torn coat in goat blood and brought it back to their father. Jacob recognized the coat, surmised had what happened, and greatly mourned the loss of his favored son.

The traders took Joseph to Egypt and sold him as a slave to Potiphar, one of Pharaoh's officials. The Bible tells us the Lord was with Joseph, prospering him in his Egyptian master's house (Genesis 39:2). He was entrusted with great responsibility to run the household and oversee Potiphar's holdings. Even during the time Joseph was imprisoned after Potiphar's wife falsely accused him of attempting to rape her, the Lord remained with him, putting him in good standing with the chief jailer. He was placed in charge of the prisoners and the entire jail, completely without supervision. God made sure everything went well for Joseph.

While in prison, Joseph interpreted dreams for the king's cupbearer and baker, both imprisoned for offending their master. Each interpretation was prophetic. He asked them to remember this and mention him to Pharaoh when they got out of prison. Upon release, the chief cupbearer was restored to his post, but the chief baker was hanged. Two years later, as Pharaoh puzzled over two troubling dreams, the chief cupbearer finally remembered to mention Joseph.

Pharaoh sent for him, then eagerly listened to Joseph's understanding of his dreams. First, giving God all the credit for his interpretations, he explained they were related and foretold Egypt's future of seven years of abundant harvest, followed by seven years of famine. These dreams let Pharaoh know God's plan in advance, so he could prepare for it all to unfold. Pharaoh was so impressed with Joseph that he put this young man in charge of his palace and all of Egypt. As with every situation he had been in, Joseph used his leadership and administrative skills, saving the Egyptian people from famine. God's favor remained with him.

After the seven years of famine began, Jacob sent ten of his sons to buy grain in Egypt. Joseph didn't immediately reveal his identity to his brothers in their dealings, but when he did, he told them everything had happened according to God's plan to save lives (Genesis 45:4-6). He instructed his brothers to return with Jacob, and their relational restoration began (Genesis 45:9-24). The family was reunited when they moved to Egypt.

Years later, Jacob became ill and died. All the brothers and family joined in mourning his death. The brothers worried that Joseph would treat them badly in retaliation for all they had done. Since he was now in such a powerful position, they believed they were sure to get what was due them. They sent a message to Joseph detailing their father's request to forgive them. When they came to see him, they threw themselves down before him. He assured them he held no ill will, instead promising to continue to provide for them, explaining his forgiveness for what they had done (Genesis 50:19-21):

Joseph replied, "Don't be afraid. Do I act for God? Don't you see, you planned evil against me, but God used those same plans for my good, as you see all around you right now—life for many people. Easy now, you have nothing to fear; I'll take care of you and your children." He reassured them, speaking with them heart-to-heart.

There are many takeaways in this story:
- God is in control, using even bad things for our good.
- God has plans for us and promises to prosper us.
- Nothing can divert us from God's purpose.
- God is always with us, in good times and bad.
- Forgiveness and restoration are possible; they may take a lifetime to achieve.
- Forgiveness is based on love and truth, offered in obedience to God.
- Forgiveness is releasing someone from doing wrong, with no grudge held nor debt owed.
- When grace is extended, all are freed from bondage and can freely move forward.
- Forgiveness allows us to begin again.

Getting There is the Thing

We are all blessed beyond measure. Remember His mercy:

Now that we are set right with God by means of this sacrificial death, the consummate blood sacrifice, there is no longer a question of being at odds with God in any way. If, when we were at our worst, we were put on friendly terms with God by the sacrificial death of his Son, now that we're at our best, just think of how our lives will expand and deepen by means of his resurrection life! Now that we have actually received this amazing friendship with God, we are no longer content to simply say it in plodding prose. We sing and shout our praises to God through Jesus, the Messiah! (Romans 5:9-11)

Forgiveness happens like this:
- Because we have been forgiven by accepting Christ as our Lord and Savior, we are reconciled to God, through Jesus.
- All are offered this wonderful gift before becoming a believer (Christ follower).
- This offer is available to anyone willing to accept it, even to those we have not yet reconciled with.
- Christians are to live in love, forgive others, and extend grace as often as needed.
- As we are all still reconciled in Him, what's holding up our painful relational restoration (with professed believers or not)? The answer is simple: us.

Maybe you believe the well has been poisoned for you to do the things you want, to accomplish something truly remarkable, concluding you're just not worthy or capable. You're sure you have no chance of making what you hope to happen, because someone has set traps or made it difficult for you. Joseph's story clearly illustrates the fact that if what we pray to do is part of God's plan for us, it's going to happen.

So, don't fear the dreaded rejection notice, being turned down for that dream job, or failing to create a beautiful life with someone you love. There is one letter of difference in the words dread and dream. But the difference between the two words is much bigger than just one letter. It is God. He makes all the difference.

Remember, the Lord was (and is) with me (and you). It's remarkable what can be accomplished through Him, against all odds by the world's standards. But the world's standards are not God's. His are expansive, inclusive, and with a bigger view of all time. If you are willing to go with His plans, buckle your seatbelt and get ready for an incredible journey.

A True Story of Forgiveness

Some forgiveness stories last a lifetime. Consider the story of a baby girl, privately adopted before birth by a couple whose week-old daughter had died five years earlier. They loved their newly adopted daughter. Since she was uniquely chosen, her parents told her she was special. A few years later, another daughter was born to the couple, making the family complete.

Dark undercurrents in family dynamics caused continual heartbreak and sadness. The adopted daughter's special relationship eventually transformed into her becoming a scapegoat for many of her parents' own personal choices. Surrounded by loving relatives, encouraging close friends, church family, and Jesus, she endeavored to live in a way that would please her parents and make them proud of her. Unfortunately, pleasing them never happened. It was as if they never noticed. Maybe their pain was too much to bear.

Years later with her own young, growing family, her adopted family drew away. Losing family members and close friends is an incredibly painful experience. After her mother's death, the adopted daughter again experienced the loss of family a third time with her adoptive father's abandonment. Sadly, her children were never offered opportunities to have a loving relationship with him.

A longtime family friend considered adopting the girl when she was young. Instead, she remained close throughout the girl's life. In her last year of this caring friend's life, she affirmed to her (and to her family) what the girl instinctually knew, but didn't dare allow herself to feel or admit: the adopted family didn't love in the way we think a family would or should (Deuteronomy 19:5).

Even without personal experience, the girl enjoyed a close family of her own. Through physical rejection and being held apart from them, she still loved and cared about her adoptive family.

I am that adopted baby girl. I can personally attest that forgiveness for things we never understand is possible. I know for a fact that peace transcending all understanding exists on the other side of mercy. I have experienced being loved, and I have genuinely loved others unconditionally, especially when not deserved (by conventional thought) nor expected.

Are you wondering how this is possible? Are you seeking that elusive thing we call forgiveness? Let's continue on this journey as we discover more about it.

How do we forgive those who've hurt us? As we've discussed, there isn't a template or checklist to download. Our model to follow is Jesus. There are steps to take but no timetable. It takes as long as it does and maybe over the span of a lifetime—or never—to fully restore a broken relationship.

Steps to forgiving begin at the beginning, and end with "I forgive you" (all covered with prayer):

- **Acknowledge:** Give credit where credit is due for the relational break. There is always accountability. In this step, those who caused the pain are identified. Quite often, more than one person may be involved, especially when both sides have been struggling with each other. All involved in fanning the flames of discord are named. Sometimes people will deny their role in the problem or refuse to take part in attempted restoration. You can proceed without them.

- **Count the cost:** Consider what would be gained or lost by forgiving or withholding grace from someone who needs it. But please don't hit pause and hold on this step for long. As we've established, we don't have a choice to not forgive, so to wait or think otherwise is entertaining a false possibility. Thinking about what could be missed out on in life is shocking if we allow ourselves to reflect on what might be. We will never get back what we've lost, but we can begin again. The cost is in our loss, (expecting the same from others) or dogmatically forcing others to view things in our strict way is the foundation of brainwashing and dictatorial control. If this is a form of relational power, know this is a weak position that will not last outside a prescribed bubble. Personal agendas must be laid aside to move forward in the restoration process.

You can flip this picture. By taking a new angle, you can clearly see how personal differences give hurting relationships a starting point. Forgiveness begins where the differences end. People don't get to this place when they are overwhelmed and caught up with the differences they think exist. They may attempt to see their way through after they stop passing judgment. When an impasse remains, there is no toehold to move forward because they won't first erase that line in the sand.

2. Remember: Shared Purpose.

Originally, there was something that brought you together. The children? Your mother? An audacious dream or an ill-conceived scheme for greatness? Was it an inconveniently timed or forever-doomed relationship? There was a shared purpose before it all fell apart (except in cases of rape or abuse). On good days and bad, there is always shared responsibility by all (way back when and now). The eventual demise isn't completely one person's fault.

Maybe that purpose still exists and it's calling your name, imploring you not to forget. Just as differences that make life together interesting and challenging, shared purpose can be what knits us together. No matter what we think or feel, the thing that brought us together still needs us, even when we're far away from all we once knew, down the road from everything that was important to us. We may have changed in some ways, but a vestige of *us* remains.

3. Establish a Common Goal.

What's next is maybe for the children or family, or because no one is ready to rocket toward restoration. Little by little moves us forward in life as well as forgiveness. Feelings of inadequacy easily stir, considering the daunting road to restoration looming ahead. Being able to communicate a decision to continue, remaining in touch, participating at least in part in a shared life, gives hope. Jesus' light shines brightly through us in acts of coordinated free will after difficult choices are made and healing has begun.

4. Stay Focused.

Challenges will always come, but through the restorative power of working toward forgiveness, greater strength and deeper understanding develop. Hope and a desire to nurture a tender relationship keeps the focus on growing in new ways. We must face the inevitable fact that not everyone is in the same place in their life journey as we are, and their destination is not (necessarily) ours (Luke 7:47).

Understand Why Forgiveness is Important

Forgiving means extending grace to someone for doing something wrong. The wrongdoing is known and owned by the one who perpetrated the act. Grace is given with an open hand, extended to that person from a place of love, with no desire for reparation, repayment, or other strings attached. It is granted even when not deserved, and especially when never expected.

This may seem a hyper-simplified presentation of a complex topic. Admittedly, it is. However, we tend to make the process of forgiving others more difficult than it is. The result is our setting up impenetrable barriers for protection, establishing conditions making resolution nearly impossible, and living every day in continual pain. Probably one of the biggest obstacles to relational restoration and the ability to experience personal peace is having a clear understanding about what forgiveness truly is.

Let Go of That

It takes time. It may take us all the time we have remaining. At life's end, what is left behind will be our legacy. Better to depart this world leaving a trail of scattered love notes to others than unresolved bitterness in a joyless vacuum of nothingness. Feeling His influence in the midst of our meager restorative efforts fills hurting hearts with needed hope.

At some point, we all have to make a decision. A decision can be to take action or not. Not taking action is also a decision but promises to hold us in the place we wish to flee. After we make our choice, we must go with it. That is when our choice becomes a commitment as a call to take action. With a right heart and His guidance, our actions and words will be appropriate and effective.

Looking at the daunting road to restoration that looms ahead, uneasy feelings of inadequacy to deal with it all stir within us. Pray for God's guidance, wisdom, and patience in this matter. Ask Him to lead you in the ways you should go to make things right, and to bless your efforts. Pray for others involved to have willing hearts and amenable spirits to restore the relationship. Forgiving is applying grace to build a relational bridge over a troubled spot toward a better future. Rest in God's Word and know:

All this comes from God who settled the relationship between us and him, and then called us to settle our relationships with each other. (2 Corinthians 5:18)

We are called to a ministry of reconciliation. God gives us grace to endure difficult situations and to love difficult people, as He loves us. Such as we are—but all so blessed by Him—we walk in His grace.

It's difficult to comprehend that many people who seem unshakable and sure live in a constant state of self-protection mode they created themselves. Instead of living freely in God's truth and love, they have fallen for Satan's lies, which pulled them deeper into the darkness of shame, dictated by pride. They seem incapable of caring, but they are afraid, uncertain, and alone.

It's a sad truth when we think better of our malefactor or perpetrator than they do of themselves. Maybe it's because we can see the great potential they deny themselves, or pity how their life has grown so small they miss true joy and the wonder of a constant flow of positive possibilities to discover and explore.

. . .

Forgiving in Real Life: Apply the Principles and Live these Truths, Extending Grace Freely
Situation:

Sitting at a traffic light, you notice a sign on the back window of the car ahead of you: *Learning to drive stick shift. Sorry for any delays.* Remembering how it was back when you were learning to drive, you smile and settle back a bit in your seat, extending grace to the uncertain driver ahead as the light changes to green.

What if we were to give grace to others, even without a sign? Maybe someone just lost a job. Mourning the loss of their spouse? Missing their home? Aren't they equally eligible for our grace? Aren't we glad He has never withheld it from us?

Action step

Ponder this Scripture: Ephesians 2:14-22.

FIVE
FORGIVENESS MODEL

Compare and Contrast Two Forgiveness Models: The World's Ways and Jesus' Example

Comparing the worldview that shapes prevailing practices of forgiving (or not) and Jesus' example, strikes a stark contrast:

World's Ways

Focus on what was taken, respecting the bully, perpetrator, or offender. Justify wrong actions as understandable.
- Withhold forgiveness (power play for control).
- Grant forgiveness only when I deign to do so.
- Think it's quick and easy.
- Decide it's all about me and how I feel about it.
- Depend upon what I think about something.

Jesus' Example

Focus on giving grace in love, despite recognizing what was taken or wrong done by the bully, perpetrator, or offender.
- Forgive freely.
- Offer forgiveness to everyone, every day.
- Know that it's challenging.
- Follow Jesus' perfect model.
- Remember God's Word instructs and directs.

If the world's ways worked, we'd have no relational problems left unaddressed. We would abide in peace together in a civil society. These commonly applied practices shaped by the worldview do not work. Yet many Christians stubbornly ascribe to them. Why?

I pose to you, dear reader, the same question whispered to me as I struggled to write this book: "Why are you running from this?"

The world's ways have been proven ineffective. Through our own careful examination (not trying to justify previous actions), we must honestly admit these unreliable strategies are full of emotional fluff. It's similar to the light, sticky cotton candy-like stuff spun into a sickeningly sweet sugary floss around how we're feeling today. It simply candy-coats problems but never provides a satisfying solution.

So here we are, contending with complex matters requiring pure grace. It's time to wake up. It's past time to see with the eyes of our heart and forgive so we can also live free. If we never stir from this dread-filled slumber and act now, we will sleep through all that matters most. We will miss all the blessings we are yet to discover.

Why do Christians continually apply common ineffective worldview-influenced practices that are counter to their beliefs?
- Not understanding what forgiveness is.
- Not accurately applying the principle of forgiveness in daily life, just as Jesus has done for us.

- Not fully understanding the precepts of mercy and how they relate to every misstep we encounter.
- Not living up to the high standards God has laid out, instructing us to live in forbearance with one another.
- Seeking a quick, easy answer to a problem, versus acting in a principled manner—a hallmark of Christian life—is difficult.

Couple any combination of the above (or more) reasons with the fact that forgiveness can be difficult—paired with understanding personal nuances to rightly embrace wrong practices—and the result is an unobstructed view of how we got to this place. Unfortunately, the bumpy road to forgiveness is filled with bottlenecks, misunderstandings, and littered with broken hearts along the way.

As we continue to bobble and squirm in our tormenting sea of adversity, getting our arms around this appears to be an exhausting impossibility. But if it were so easy to repair relationships on our own, we wouldn't need Jesus, would we?

Our Grace Daily Challenge

Life presents daily opportunities to forgive and receive forgiveness. Moment by moment, every grace upon grace is showered down on us, by our loving God. He does so quite thoroughly, and yet in our own messes, we struggle with it.

Maybe we struggle with a menacing thorny issue that has transformed into a throbbing reality. It relentlessly disrupts our daily activity. Perhaps a shocking personal discovery of a wrong committed by someone close rips through our heart with tornadic prowess. It is set on a course determined to dismantle life as we know it.

The Bible says we need not worry, nor live with regret, mourning what should have been:

Don't fret or worry. Instead of worrying, pray. Let petitions and praises shape your worries into prayers, letting God know your concerns. Before you know it, a sense of God's wholeness, everything coming together for good, will come and settle you down. It's wonderful what happens when Christ displaces worry at the center of your life. (Philippians 4:6-7)

Through forgiveness, we surrender all that is thrust upon us, releasing its hold. To withhold grace allows any interference to steer our future off-course, veering away from following our loving Father's plan for our life. Daily living with an "if only" state of mind instead of in the blessed now, creates an empty void in our heart that will likely never be filled. Allowing another control over us—whether a person, situation, or pervading thought—promises that we will miss out on God's best for our life (Galatians 4:7).

As believers, we are to follow Jesus' example. Detailed throughout the Bible, we can see He extended grace easily and frequently. The Bible says:

Be even-tempered, content with second place, quick to forgive an offense. Forgive as quickly and completely as the Master forgave you." (Colossians 3:13-14a).

For humans, forgiveness may not come easily, and we know it doesn't come often enough. Looking at God's model through Jesus helps us understand what it's about, and how to live life with a forgiving spirit.

Forgiveness Begins with God's Love

Countless people worldwide—professed Christians as well as those who are not—are familiar with the Bible verse John 3:16:

This is how much God loved the world: He gave his Son, his one and only Son. And this is why: so that no one need be destroyed; by believing in him, anyone can have a whole and lasting life.

. . .

This important verse is emphasized so frequently, I admit failing to read much beyond it very often. In not reading John 3 further for deeper meaning, I nearly missed grasping a firm understanding of God's full intent in sacrificing his Son Jesus Christ on our behalf:

God didn't go to all the trouble of sending his Son merely to point an accusing finger, telling the world how bad it was. He came to help, to put the world right again. Anyone who trusts in him is acquitted; anyone who refuses to trust him has long since been under a death sentence without knowing it. And why? Because of that person's failure to believe in the one-of-a-kind Son of God when introduced to him. (John 3:17-18)

I wonder how many others have missed this glimpse of God's divine forgiveness in action. In studying this passage, we can see God already knew we were a troubled people needing His help. Instead of telling us how we were all completely hopeless (without Jesus) and helpless (without God) miserable individuals, He came to earth in human form and showed us how to live and forgive by providing a way through His son Jesus Christ.

If all this were not enough, He provided us not only the Truth (His Holy Word) to guide us, and a Light (Jesus) to help us see, but also a Way (salvation) through His forgiveness of our sins by confessing them to Him and accepting Jesus as our Lord and Savior. God loves all of us. He wants a forever relationship with each of us. Through His restoration at our every broken place, this can happen. Through our salvation and with the Holy Spirit living within us, we have the power to forgive.

God is in this relationship with us for the long haul. His desire for closer ties with us is not just for today or the things we'll be doing next year. It isn't because we're an awesome person who makes incredible things happen, or we're just plain fun to watch. It's because He loves us so much and wants us to keep Him in our lives forever. In fact, He wants to restore all the brokenness in our lives, which is available through His forgiveness. He wants us to live with Him in heaven for eternity. Jesus told his disciples in John 14:1-4:

Don't let this throw you. You trust God, don't you? Trust me. There is plenty of room for you in my Father's home. If that weren't so, would I have told you that I'm on my way to get a room ready for you? And if I'm on my way to get your room ready, I'll come back and get you so you can live where I live. And you already know the road I'm taking.

Considering all God has done and is actively doing in the lives of His people, He apparently has a plan for all of us (Ephesians 2:10). Human nature promises ongoing slips and falls. Our meager efforts are insufficient to face any battle on our own. Life experience shows us we are not able to safely navigate life's turbulent waters alone. He always keeps His promises and said we would never be alone. God's gift of forgiveness is wrapped in His love.

Following Jesus' Example

God provides our every need, including how to forgive. Relationships are maintained by making amends where necessary. Living with love, in mutual respect, is essential. Through unity, we can stand as one, living together in a bond of peace. It is the coming together of individuals with the same heart, joined with the express purpose of reconciling, nurturing, or maintaining their relationship.

This type of relationship is forged between individuals who have matured in life. They understand loving, encouraging, and caring for one another is far more important than understanding *why* something happened as it did. Accurately identifying and explaining away another's quirks and challenges in life is not required. It is never expecting agreement on all issues, nor walking in lockstep on all viewpoints.

Being mature is not necessarily determined by the number of years we have lived. It is developed through living with forbearance as we extend grace and peace to others in the midst of personal messes and any chaos created by others. It's not calling someone out or shunning them for personal convenience, nor publicly flogging them for what they did. It's not carrying the weight of another's wrong around with you for the rest of your days.

It's realizing this is part of the humanness of everyone who lives and has ever lived. It's understanding that all of us are specially gifted, but also indelibly flawed in some ways. By recognizing the irrefutable fact no one is perfect, the way is made clear in obvious conclusion: we're all in this together.

Every person is a unique individual. Each of us embraces our own standards and lives by closely held truths that guide every moment of our lives. Living in grace and peace with others doesn't require selling-out personal convictions or compromising beliefs to more comfortably accommodate another's diverging viewpoint or lifestyle. Taking a close look at our own heart, attitudes, and behaviors is the starting point toward building common ground. Once established, this is the foundation upon which restored relationships will comfortably rest.

Perhaps you're reading this book, looking for answers because you've already tried all that. You have lived this way, but another in a close relationship did not. It was devastating. Maybe you've been falsely accused. Someone you held dear deceived you in an incredibly hurtful way or you were abandoned. How can you go on living in grace and peace? How can you forgive such undeserved acts?

Because a perplexing situation feels unapproachable, it seems there is no simple answer. A solution may not come quickly. Our hurt develops ever-tightening tentacles that wrap around the tender heart, squeezing. It dramatically changes our world as we knew and lived it in previously unimaginable ways. It feels as if we're suffocating. Daily dread and anguish invade. The pain runs rampant, spreading to all corners of life, with roots so deep a standard pre-packaged treatment or over-the-counter remedy will never repair this wound. A radical approach with intentional, surgical precision is required. The Bible says (Deuteronomy 30:6):

God, your God, will cut away the thick calluses on your heart and your children's hearts, freeing you to love God, your God, with your whole heart and soul and live, really live.

Only the Lord can effectively treat our hearts, freeing us to love Him while creating within us a forgiving spirit. In this sacred operation performed through the miracle of His grace, He removes moral delinquencies and cleans up impurities found in the site of His incision. This essential procedure of God's forgiveness is performed at the spiritual level. The only way for this to occur is to look to Him. No personal checklist, framework, or system we devise or attempt to work though can accomplish what He can do within us.

This measure is what it takes for us to live in love and peace, freely extending grace amidst the chaos. To live otherwise permits that hurting, hateful thing to take precedence in life by allowing it to rule. This risk causes us to delay any reconciliation and forfeit our rightful claim to overcome it. For as long as we leave room for it in our life, we will stay stuck at this roadblock, separated from a joy-filled existence.

In so doing, we unnecessarily lose the joys God intends for His children by relinquishing them to another desiring to claim them for no good reason. This will be done entirely at the expense of present and future joy, happy memories, family or friends, or life adventures we will never experience as a result. We rob ourselves of decades of what could be beautiful memories to hold forever in our heart, shared with those near and dear.

The Imperative Need for Forgiveness

Upon completion, the canvas upon which our life is painted will have shockingly blank spaces. Life for those with an unforgiving spirit (or unwillingness to step forward to make things right) will be as if all the celebrations and happy times never happened. At the terrible moment of realization, we acknowledge inadvertently drinking that poison after all.

Fortunately, if you did imbibe that fatal drink, it's not too late to change course. Fear not. As our human nature is, many have tasted it and survived through God's grace.

There are numerous reasons why it is imperative for victims and those wronged to work through issues to regain control over their lives. This is essential for applying forgiveness where needed. Counter to the worldview, withholding forgiveness is proven as an unsuccessful strategy for closure. If withholding forgiveness worked, there would be no need to seek restoration. We would experience no ongoing pain or relational troubles. It is obvious that none of the world's ways are working, no matter how we spin it. Relationship is not all about *me*.

By not forgiving, the sufferer remains attached to the distressing matter for as long as they choose to take no further action in making things right. Taking a small step toward restoration or extending grace requires a change in a victim's life to accept the control they have within themselves through the indwelling Holy Spirit to forgive.

This may be daunting to those who feel they have little control over their own lives. They may not like life as it is now, but fear entering unfamiliar territory. Not knowing how life might be after efforts to repair the broken places are initiated can create an overwhelming feeling of immobilization. A change in heart is required, including a strong desire to live the life God wants for His children.

There are measures to be taken in forgiving, but God has not provided a precise timetable or effective five-step success formula for reaching absolution. No push-button gadget or mobile app for resolving matters of the heart exists. There is no life hack for fixing the mess like a ninja. Working through our challenges is as unique as is every individual and their circumstances.

Maybe that's one of the points of extending grace. We must solve each of these problematic breaks one at a time. In so doing, we consider the relationship and how best to resolve the issues. An issue may be quickly resolved. Sometimes, grace for an offense may be granted many years later, gratefully received, or given at life's end—or never.

Misshaped matters of the heart are uncomfortable. Realizing the tremendous personal risk involved in taking necessary steps toward repair stirs deep fears. Actions taken to rectify a situation do not promise the outcome will be as hoped. Not having a guarantee of complete success in fixing life's messes makes this even more daunting.

While we can never know what tomorrow will bring us, this should never keep us from attempting to move toward forgiveness. There is always something that can be done. Directly applying this soothing balm over a wound promotes healing. There is still hope. We can always move forward with the hope of making things better.

Moving Forward

I've come to this place as I think about how I've extended forgiveness throughout my life. Maybe—hopefully—you have too. Perhaps like me, you've had frequent occasions to search for forgiveness within, for inflicted injury both great and small. Amid turbulence experienced throughout our life journey we all have opportunities to bestow grace and to receive it. Possibly, we have sought forgiveness as well. Most of us never ask for absolution enough. None of it is easy.

Even when attempting to live in peace with others, things happen that result from human interaction and related reaction. Regretted words are spoken, evil thoughts are shared, and illogical, reckless, even malicious acts are perpetrated upon others, creating discord, harm, and disconnect.

Similar to the clean-up crew after a riot, the rectifying effort can begin immediately, clearing through the wreckage with sustaining vigilance. In life, every type of situation requiring focused attention exists, each in a different stage concerning forgiveness. To live a life with positive impact, we must endeavor to see these matters through to the fullest extent of possible resolution. Only then are we able to live freely, releasing the encumbrances and entrapments we would otherwise drag along with us for as long as we allow.

In attempting to live a grace-filled life, we can live a life of joy. Is life perfect? No. But it offers us the possibility to be freed of obstacles that otherwise crowd out living life. Does this mean we promote ourselves to the position of judge, declaring a case-by-case ruling? No, because judging isn't a part of forgiveness. It is merely an extension of an unforgiving spirit. It promotes finding and focusing on another's faults instead of seeking a peaceful resolution and a way forward.

Placing judgment upon another or withholding pardon for any wrongdoing keeps us from moving forward to a place of freedom. I've been on this trail a long time. Our hope, peace, and future rest entirely on forgiveness. The first step is forgiving ourselves and accepting God's forgiveness of our wrongs by embracing the priceless gift of salvation wrapped in His love and delivered through His Son, Jesus Christ. He sees us as worthy. This everyday essential helps frame things with an accurate perspective. It needs to be carried with us at all times. Once released from our constraints, this is the way to fully live life, with the joy and peace we desire. We hold the keys.

The Ultimate Example

God is the definitive example of forgiveness. The picture He paints of unconditional love is the most astonishing the world has ever seen. It is so different from anything we know that fully understanding it is mind-blowing.

How would you react if someone killed a family member or very close friend? What if someone raped your daughter, mother, or sister? After the tragic incident, would you extend an invitation for that perpetrator to come live with you, in your house? Of course, most people wouldn't. Human logic, emotion, and understanding don't permit us to make such an outlandish offer. But God made an incredible offer to everyone. He sent his only son to share the Good News with mankind, personally delivering His gracious invitation to come live with them in heaven (where there is no sin)—and then we killed Jesus.

But God's son rose from the dead, and His invitation remains open to all people in this world who will accept it. He stands ready to receive each of us, waiting with open arms to welcome us home to live with Him. He means what He says. His offer is a firm, reliable, unchanging promise, no matter what we have done or how we've lived our lives.

While we can quickly detect even the slightest imperfection within ourselves and in others, elaborating on all the wrongs done to hurt us sometimes seems as natural as breathing. This is not the path toward forgiveness. Following God's time-tested model illustrated by Jesus shows us real relationship-building, and forgiving is the only way to build lasting connections. His way may seem counterintuitive to our little minds, but His way works because He begins the restoration process at the heart of every matter.

God sees our value even when we don't. He wants to restore and maintain a relationship with us. As His children, we are family. He is the beginning of our tie with all. We are wired for this. Deep down, everyone knows this instinctually, whether we consciously acknowledge or reject this reality. Some choose to ignore this. Regrettably, others may never accept it, continuing their futile quest seeking what they do not know.

Following His model of forgiveness is the pathway of release from self-imposed and situational bindings. These are obstacles that keep us from needed physical, mental, spiritual, and emotional freedom. God's cup of mercy is the ultimate bottomless cup.

Many good things are possible and intended for us by Him. Why would we not want to receive every good thing He has for us? By acting on our own, effectively leaving Him out of the picture, we will not be rightful beneficiaries of all His incredible blessings.

Our God is a loving Father. He wants what is best for us. Scripture assures He has a plan for each of us (Hebrews 11:40). We must be willing participants, not just someone standing by, impatiently waiting with open hands to receive. He has given us free will for choosing. Our freedom is not limited. When we make our own way without Him, it's just that—ours. It's a hollow existence, barren in times of reaping reward because our own way is never as fruitful as God's.

Our special relationship includes times when we find it difficult to forgive ourselves for something we've done. Maybe personal disappointments make it impossible to get past. Release from our strangleholds is available by taking them to Him in prayer, asking for guidance and help to work our way through. While it is possible to build our own prisons and remain incarcerated indefinitely, it is impossible to break free of this stronghold under our own power.

Jesus assured us of our need to trust in and rely on God in Matthew 19:26:

Jesus looked hard at them and said, "No chance at all if you think you can pull it off yourself. Every chance in the world if you trust God to do it."

Loving the unlovable is not done through well-placed words or a burst of feelings, but through intentional deeds. It's easy to nurse a grudge and simple to justify relationship. In doing so, we live in a state that paralyzes our ability to forgive, trapping all involved. Instead, we must live above the situation and love beyond it, even amidst relational turmoil or problems. Compassion is the only way we can live forward through the troubling matter with confidence as we make necessary efforts to move toward restoration.

Sometimes we become confused in the rough and tumble of the chaos. Confusion leaves us wondering what to do and how to handle troubling matters. Jesus gives clear counsel in Matthew 7:12:

Here is a simple, rule-of-thumb guide for behavior: Ask yourself what you want people to do for you, then grab the initiative and do it for them. Add up God's Law and Prophets, and this is what you get.

Scripture reminds us that while we are all sinners (unlovable at best), God forgave us. He extends mercy, grace, peace, and love to all. In the aftermath of receiving His forgiveness as part of rebuilding a relationship with Him—with hopeful prayers to help clean up our mess—a few small vestiges may surface in the rubble.

These are haunting reminders of the enveloping darkness that just dissipated. Don't linger in this place for long, reviewing and remembering each one of them. Clear the way forward and burn that garbage.

Following God's model of forgiveness, we relinquish our choice to remember what He has chosen to forget. In our own small human minds and tiny hearts, we may otherwise decide to cling to those scraps, building yet another blockade, never able to move from that place.

Awareness of Sin

What about sins committed unintentionally or in ignorance? We may not be aware of all our sins, but the Lord sees every one of them. Not judging on the spot, He washes each away, cleansing us all of our sin (Numbers 15:25). Following Jesus' example, we are called to extend grace to those who may unknowingly or unintentionally offend or hurt us. As we come to know the person better, we may learn they would never have meant to hurt anyone. We might discover they would be embarrassed to know their actions caused harm.

Sometimes, people's actions are unexpected and unexplainable. Maybe what they've done is not in keeping with who they are as we know them. Covering them with grace, we pray for them. In faith, we must be willing to leave the matter at Jesus' feet. If we truly let go of the matter, it is possible to maintain a relationship with someone needing the loving care we can provide this side of heaven (Matthew 24:22).

Relationships require nurturing. They take deliberate effort and unsung courage. We can be effective in caring for relationships when we live a life that is open to addressing the needs of others through faith, with emotional integrity.

Once we become aware of this unfilled need and fully accept a new way of life, it can become as natural as breathing. To follow through day by day, compassionately tending relationships is a selfless desire to nourish and enrich the lives of others. It is a sincere desire to want what is best and be willing to do what it takes to ensure a positive impact. This is accomplished by accepting to live as Jesus did, blessing others through loving actions.

Who Pays the Cost?

In a recent discussion about forgiveness, a faithful Christian friend confided they believed the one who forgives always bears the cost of extending grace. As with all conversations I've had with people while writing this book, I listened respectfully to hear the hurting heart speak, but my restless spirit wanted to burst out immediately to point out the inaccuracy of this limiting belief. I held back, knowing this was a divine appointment to show me yet another perspective I needed to hear and address in this book.

As Christians, our beliefs shape how we regard forgiveness. If we're not careful, we may not be as closely aligned to Scripture and how God views grace as we might think. It's easy to fool ourselves into believing we have this all figured out while still struggling to apply it in our lives.

Case-in-Point

Remember when I admitted not reading much beyond the often-quoted John 3:16 verse? I've read the Bible through twice, but by not reacquainting myself with the two verses that follow (John 3:17-18), I could easily miss out on two necessary ingredients for extending grace as I try to follow Jesus' example of forgiveness.

Those essentials are:
- Not placing judgment on others (this is God's role, as it clearly says in this passage).
- Trusting Him in all things.

This means whatever we think of another (including what they did to us or why), delivering judgment is not our job and will undoubtedly serve only as an obstacle to our living and making things right. Our efforts must be based on trusting in and relying on God alone.

Still, thoughts of the future can be terrifying. We wonder what will become of those who've done us wrong. What will our life be like when the dust settles? Will we still see this person? What will our relationship be like? These unknowns are foreboding, but we need not let that hold us back. We can rest in knowing God has that handled too. In Deuteronomy 30:7-9, we're assured:

God, your God will put all these curses on your enemies who hated you and were out to get you. And you will make a new start, listening obediently to God, keeping all his commandments that I'm commanding you today. God, your God will outdo himself in making things go well for you: you'll have babies, get calves, grow crops, and enjoy an all-round good life. Yes, God will start enjoying you again, making things go well for you just as he enjoyed doing it for your ancestors.

You may be wondering about this biblical reference and how it applies to us today, especially after Jesus Christ came to earth and died on the cross for God's forgiveness of our sins. This verse shows God's real intent and timeless promise for His children. He made good on it for the Israelites, and He has every intention of keeping His promise in fulfilling His plans in our lives as well.

Regardless of how frightening it may be to think of dealing with any painful or embarrassing matters that require our attention and grace, isn't is encouraging to know our "God will outdo himself in making things go well" for us? We get a new start—a fresh beginning. We have the possibility of enjoying an all-round good life. Try as we may, we cannot do this on our own. We can move to a new area or get a new job, but we take the existing issues with us. We can run from a problem, but like Jonah spit back on land by the whale, we cannot avoid it.

Only God can make all things new. As we let go through our forgiveness and trust in Him, we can rebuild and strengthen our relationship with our Father. Scripture says, "God will start enjoying you again, making things go well for you just as he enjoyed doing it for your ancestors." A relationship is what He wants with us. Our plights and concerns are opportunities to receive His blessing if we permit it.

So, in answer to any question (or feeling) about who pays the cost in forgiving: *Jesus paid it all.*

A Blatant Case for Forgiveness

Throughout Lent, we are reminded of Jesus' mockery as a part of the suffering inflicted upon Him by Judas, the chief priests and scribes, Herod, and guards horrid indignities. He was treated as worthless and despicable, ridiculed, taunted ... and then He was crucified.

Never has there been a more blatant case for forgiveness and unexpected grace. It was not sought nor expected by the majority who were convinced they were right—when they were so wrong—when Jesus was crucified. Even so, all are generously lavished with grace. That offer to all is a sealed promise. It still stands today for anyone who accepts Jesus' invitation.

For some, each day is clouded by being treated as unworthy,

placed there forever by other members of society, groups, or families. Those closest may choose a lifelong label for the cursed for not being as fast, smart, better, or beautiful.

Maybe the maligned is perceived as *better* by those harboring ill will. Perhaps the detractor wants to unseat their rival because they believe the blessing is undeserved. Jealousy may drive the harsh punishment of someone appropriately using their God-given gifts and—worse yet—in their confused minds, succeeding (Psalm 22:7).

As mentioned in chapter two, there are endless stories of mental, emotional, physical, and spiritual abuse. When we experience treatment like this, loving more is the best answer, difficult as that may seem. It can take a long time to get to that place.

This shocking principle is vividly illustrated by Jesus loving beyond measure as He underwent horrific torture that even by today's standards most would agree was extreme. By dying on the cross, Jesus paid ahead for the forgiveness of all sins committed by anyone in this world willing to believe in Him. This is an inclusive offer extended freely and for all who will accept it.

This reminds us of the importance of forgiveness in all matters. Even if we can't express it directly to the person (for reasons of personal safety or they are deceased), it is still possible. It's important. It's shown in love. Even if the person we want to forgive desires to remain imprisoned in their unforgiving world, we don't have to stay there. We have the key. That key is love.

We can never go wrong embracing what is right according to God's high standards and principles. Following Jesus' example, we need to forgive freely, trusting in Him. All things are possible through Him (Matthew 19:26). God blesses us beyond imagination for doing hard things. He brings us through the times we want most to avoid, and we grow closer to Him.

It's plain to see God is all about relationships and delights when we fellowship with Him. Certainly, we can agree His ways are not the world's ways. Throughout my scriptural research in writing this book, I never saw references to the forgiveness process, prescribed steps, or specified conditions for extending grace to others. I saw God's principles applied broadly, lived out by Jesus.

Relationships are unique. Each one consists of individuals with their own set of beliefs, passions, and differing viewpoints. Because humans are involved, any resulting difficulties cannot be mended by following a standardized step-by-step process, using a man-created template or checklist. Yet mankind still creates systems and multifaceted procedures intended to make things happen in our own way. God has created all, and His will is done. By following His precepts and wisdom, we can, in time, smooth the otherwise rough way to absolution through a personal approach.

Our own forays into fixing things systematically have been proven as impractical in solving relational problems. While forgiving isn't easy, His ways simplify addressing difficult situations. Seeking His guidance first helps us to see more clearly. His perfect standards and principles are time-tested, always appropriate, and effective in all situations. Realizing the salvation received, grace freely chooses to forgive, passing the gift on for a better future.

One More Thing

What about those who don't know Him? Those who create chaos and perpetrate maliciousness in the lives of believers? God has always promised to use wrong for His good. We know He does.

We might be the only person on earth to show grace to the lost person who hurt us. It is a sight to behold, giving others cause to wonder, how it's possible to show grace under fire during such trying times, forgiving the pain inflicted. How can it be?

Where there is love, there is hope. Where love and hope abound, there is grace. Forgiveness makes way for endless joy and inexplicable peace.

The grace of our Lord Jesus Christ is abundant. And it is offered to all people. He is the ultimate illustration of forgiveness and endless grace. His life of unconditional love serves as a model for us to grant forgiveness to all. We prove our need for Jesus' grace and peace repeatedly in our daily lives. As His followers, we are to live by His example, embrace His teachings, and apply His instruction.

Forgiving in Real Life: Apply the Principles and Live these Truths by Personal Challenge

Are you a Christian sitting here reading these words, feeling as if you already know all of this? Good. Let the forgiveness you seek begin with you.

Action Step

How will you show forgiveness today?

SIX
FORGIVING THE OFFENSE

Unpleasant incidents create unnecessary chaos in life. Too big to ignore for long, the tangled mess captures our attention. It quickly transforms into a pulsating and undesirable issue crying out to be addressed.

Torment comes in many forms. It may touch us in the most intimate ways. Those who know us best hurl pain-causing offenses in our direction. Sometimes it is delivered simply by our chance encounters in everyday life.

Emotional wounds, like crime scene push marks on a victim shoved off a cliff, are nearly impossible to notice. While imperceptible to most people's eyes, the traces remain.

In the world, we observe things happening we will never understand. Horrific atrocities, unwarranted hatred, and irreconcilable differences add obstacles that litter our way to living a peace-filled life. When the unthinkable intrudes into our lives, we helplessly believe we must choose how to handle it.

Maybe our world is unexpectedly rocked by offensive actions against everything we believe. We watch the unmerciful torturing of innocents. Every hateful incident hurts the human heart. Incomprehensible as it may seem to be, all these things (and other possibilities) are matters requiring forgiveness.

The truth is every moment of every day provides an ongoing need for extending grace, ranging from a small slight to the highest offense. It may not take as much effort to forgive minor matters, but forgiving major issues takes time.

Forgiveness is not a simple issue. The way to grace is fraught with challenges and confusion. Common misconceptions further muddy the turbulent waters. Today's pop psychology actively encourages abuse victims to withhold extending absolution to their perpetrators. Widely promoted as an empowering strategy for those preyed upon, this faulty counsel misleads them into falsely believing they gain personal power and maintain control over their evildoers. Instead, sufferers remain chained to their transgressor until they choose to release this painful bondage by cutting the tie that binds them. This is only done through forgiveness. The world's lies offer empty promises of an altered state of reality that can never exist.

This is a prevailing example of the world's lies telling hurting people what they want to hear based on an entirely different (false) view of truth and reality. In this case, a means to gain control over a complicated matter while reducing personal pain is touted as the way. Who wouldn't want that?

It's reassuring to think our own retribution for wrongs committed is swift and final. We readily adopt this strategy because it feeds our desire for control. Accomplishing it is our personal win for moving on and living life. It's a quick and easy solution to an annoying problem. Once we get around to reviewing an issue and either stuffing it somewhere in the background or packing it away for the power it gives, feels like a done-and-won process.

Such misguided thinking is based on the belief that ending this pain can be accomplished effortlessly by doing nothing more than acknowledging an issue's generalities and then putting a lid on it. Breathing a sigh of relief, we mistakenly think we are freed from it and can leave this matter behind.

The world has a way of blurring sin's rough edges for egregious wrongs committed. Even in cases of proven personal damage, conditional leniency is applied at personal whim. This can sway the favor to the perpetrator's advantage. Saying something done is a *little* wrong is a feeble attempt to soften its blow. It sounds better, doesn't it? But the fact is the incident happened, and the pain is real.

Explaining away *why* something happened as it did is the world's way of banishing a disturbing truth. It is a weak strategy to resolve a recognized issue without rendering the earned punishment. Apologizing for a wrongdoer as if he or she is still a small child not yet in full control of their actions, only attempts to rationalize that no harm was ever intended. This is an attempt to dilute the grievous wrong committed by reasoning it isn't really as terrible as we might otherwise believe. It is an unacceptable excuse wrapped and delivered in compassionate-sounding words, sealed with the purpose of misdirecting all from the truth.

Understanding Forgiveness

There is much more to forgiveness than we know. When we ignore problems in our relationships, we let others control the relationship. It acknowledges their greater authority overall and gives control to one party to maintain all aspects of the relationship. By sitting back, never expressing a desire to repair a broken place, we give our permission for it to remain in disrepair.

Aren't we grateful our Father loves us so dearly? Isn't it comforting to think that as broken as we are, He will restore the shattered pieces of our lives and heal our hurts with His love and infinite grace?

In John 3:16-17, the Bible tells us:
This is how much God loved the world: He gave his Son, his one and only Son. And this is why: so that no one need be destroyed; by

believing in him, anyone can have a whole and lasting life. God didn't go to all the trouble of sending his Son merely to point an accusing finger, telling the world how bad it was. He came to help, to put the world right again.

In carefully reviewing this Scripture, we see God acted in love. Notice that the second half of this passage tells us God didn't send Jesus to die on the cross for our salvation to show us how wrong we are. He took this strong action to help us and set the world right again. It was selfless and all done in love. God's unconditional love and unlimited grace are our ultimate models for forgiveness.

Romans 3:23 reminds us that everyone has sinned and fallen short of God's glory. Humans are a fickle lot. We busy ourselves with things that matter most to us in the present moment. It seems there is always something requiring more of our attention. We fully believe our activity leads us to maintain a life filled with purpose. *Busy* has become revered as a public sign showing others that we live a life of value and great importance. But the truth is every life has value, and everyone living has something of significance to add to the world.

We might measure our daily accomplishments by seeing the quantity and perceived weight of priority items checked-off our to-do list. It feels good to get things done, but this busyness leads to distraction from life's most important gifts. To determine if you're living by the numbers, review daily lists to see how many people you've included, desiring to be in touch with them, in the hope of building and restoring relationships.

We, or someone crossing our path, will need grace. Maybe upon dispensing a pardon as we strive to restore a broken relationship, we consider the forgiveness process completed, which frees everyone to move on. Because we tend to live in the moment, it's easy to forget ongoing grace and care is essential to nurture and maintain healthy relationships.

Old wounds and painful reminders can haunt our lives.

Clearly, our attempts to bury forgiveness issues is not a feasible option for living a peaceful life. No matter how we want to avoid a disturbing problem, it remains in view. Almost overnight, it grows to immense proportions. It turns into our constantly nagging companion, existing solely to annoy the fabric of our being. It hungrily gnaws at us, while feasting on our inattention. We may dare to let our minds wander into unexplored territory, wondering how to deal with this. It's easy to grow tired as our hope diminishes for realizing a peace-filled life. In the wearing-down process we admit our heart's desire is to restore a broken relationship or fix a pressing problem.

Throughout my writing this book, people have freely shared beautiful forgiveness stories with me. Each inspiring experience has given deeper insight and added greater dimension to every word. The story is in the struggle. It's telling. It's captivating.

True story

One day, fully immersed in a new, very intricate creative project, I played the if-this-then-that scenario-building mind game with myself. I was praying my way through my work but uncertain how this thing I was doing would turn out. Breaking into my deep concentration and heightening anxiety, Jesus spoke to me: "How will you be able to write about these things or help others, if you yourself don't experience them?" (Long pause...) "Trust me."

Of course He was right. I had always trusted Him, or so I thought. Maybe there were some things I just didn't bother Him with —those silly little details of lesser importance I could handle, assuming He's busy. This project was one of those that if I did it ten times, I'd done it a hundred times (slight exaggeration) over the years, so it was no big deal. Really. But this time success was critical.

I had let the fact that He is with us at all times—and wants to be involved in every aspect of our lives—slip from my needy grasp. There is no issue nor problem size requirement. It's all important to

Him. If you think about it, even the smallest decision today can have a powerful, lasting effect on the rest of our lives (John 14:1).

When I finally got over my shame and embarrassment, I asked for His forgiveness with a contrite heart. This revelation shook me. It awakened me to my reality in that moment by admitting my constant need to draw closer to Him as I follow Him ever deeper into my life's calling.

I remember His words spoken to me in late March 2016. They are now emblazoned on my heart, and I do apply them. My project turned out well, with positive results. Obviously, it was not my doing but trusting in Him completely then—and throughout the time—that made all the difference. In His great wisdom, He knew I would need to remember this going forward beyond this simple project I struggled to accomplish on my own.

It works the same way with forgiveness. Pray, seeking His guidance for courage and strength to find your way to forgiveness for others, and for yourself. He's standing by, waiting for you to trust Him in these matters.

The little girl I told you about earlier in this book (who was me) didn't let the foreboding obstacles in life get in the way of her accomplishing the things she wanted to do and felt led to do. She broke free of the pressing restraints that threatened to hold her and did the things she knew she was supposed to do.

Erase that Line in the Sand

Forgiving is a difficult concept to understand, and yet most still seek it in some way. Maybe the desire is sparked by the intent to restore a treasured relationship. Perhaps realizing the futility of it all is fueled by a strong desire to live in peace. The pain of a belabored journey may become so much that the cost involved in making a course correction is seen to be a real bargain, compared to the high personal cost of continuing to live this way.

Lingering discomfort caused by a troubling situation is further compounded by related burdens that create an unintentional drag on everyday living. Humans have an innate desire to live unfettered and free. Constraints, restrictions, and if-this-then-that formulaic living are foreign to most who want to live seamlessly like a ninja in the flow. Eventually, the life cycle of this pain far outweighs the momentary inconvenience of making things right again.

To take a few steps toward re-establishing a relationship is doing something positive amidst the pervading negative energy. We may rationalize our actions as possibly getting to that place as we try to extricate ourselves from the mess. Like a carrot at the end of the stick, diminishing our pain and perhaps restoring a broken relationship we're missing becomes most important to us.

But even with the sincerest intentions, how do we move forward while the conditions that brought us all here remain? The impossibility of squaring the matter seems certain when not everyone is on board with this new approach.

Maybe the other person is still:
- Acting inappropriately.
- Living unacceptably.
- Not treating us or another properly.
- Cutting off all communication.
- Exhibiting an unwillingness to have a relationship.

First, it's essential to recognize the world offers a great deal of fluidity in permitting individual selection in their preferred state of being. This creates disorder, filling our culture with endless conflict and confusing messages. It has become the norm that ideas, feelings, and personal truths radically transform individuals as they choose to live out what they believe is their own reality, pursuing their desired lot in life. They have self-identified their entire purpose and personal role, possibly contradicting proven truths.

Perhaps the winds of chaotic change begin when we listen to that critical voice in our head. If we listen carefully, it reminds us how worthless we are, assuring us no one cares. Maybe we believe we're too fat, never skinny enough, inept, unworthy, or unattractive in every way. Perhaps the burning feeling of being *different* personally guides and directs a twisted transformation that becomes our reality.

Someone influential in our life may convince us something thought up or believed is right. Accepting it may be logical to an individual or seen as inconceivable by observers. However it is regarded, it completely changes lives forever. Perhaps embracing this new idea reshapes us to the foundations of our core being. This belief now held determines everything done from that moment onward.

Sometimes, our deepest desire or quest for something we don't have is a strong motivating factor that drives us. It may be for significant gain, a new way of living, or just becoming a new, improved *us*. Our journey focuses on that, leaving everything we believe is nonessential behind, as we move forward toward the prize.

Note these examples represent only a small sampling of possibilities that impact life direction. Changes can lead us to a better place or not, depending upon what we're thinking or feeling. But therein lies the problem. All this takes place in the murky realm of our minds, nurtured by the swirl of ever-changing feelings, steeped in emotion, and stirred by a blend of new perspectives. Through the willful distortion of truth, incongruence or disconnection from reality result, carrying us further away from others who were so dear.

In an inexhaustible quest, we may put new priorities above others while ignoring our needs. The desire for different, more, better, and greater notoriety is never totally satisfied. Instead, it develops into a cavernous hole that can never be filled. With every measured scoop, it only continues to voraciously widen, creeping to massive proportions.

To honestly recognize possibilities—while we examine established truths as well as fallacies—gives a better understanding as to how we arrived at this place. Maybe a light now shines on the broken pieces of our hard relationships. Perhaps we can see how the unforgiving ones in our life may have helped us dig that hole. It may be shocking to hear, but we are all in this together, and there's no getting out of it on our own.

Fortunately for all of us, understanding everything that surrounds or causes troubled relationships is not required to repair them. Our futile attempts to make sense of things that don't, serve only as a decoy to any progress toward resolution. We can spend a lifetime trying to wrap our mind around a projected rationale, which brings us right back to where we began this sojourn so long ago.

Sorting matters out this way is futile because we apply our brand of knowledge and logic to an emotionally fueled and senseless act. This natural inclination may be a momentary comfort. Possibly, it makes us feel superior because we sense a perceived upper hand over the issue. We may feel we have greater control by determining causes and reasons—even applying labels—but possible scenarios are endless. We may never guess correctly. We will never have all the information or know the other's truth behind the mess. Our keenest perspective of any situation is simply our own view.

Look around. Labels and logic never answer the world's problems. Instead, they encourage them through permissive division, discrimination, and disparaging others as a class or identified group of people. Caring people are able to work toward restoration. To be free, we need to roll up our sleeves and be willing to address forgiveness issues to the fullest extent possible, within our capabilities.

Why Bother to Forgive?

Do you ever feel it's easier to limit your time with someone you sense is threatening or looking for good dirt to share? Do you sometimes attempt to avoid crossing paths with someone you believe is difficult? In today's fast-paced life marred by long-held misunderstandings, we easily convince ourselves it's desirable to remain in a place of security and comfort, a safe distance from further harm and hurt.

This protection is our mistaken belief that challenging issues can be successfully held off at arm's length. We are never separated from what has happened or what exists, because a matter affecting our inner life remains. Unresolved issues persist, silently festering like a malignancy in our spirit. The focus of our daily life may turn to devise ways of avoiding a stressful situation or unbearably feisty person. Like misguided victims withholding forgiveness, we remain bound to painful circumstances we wish to avoid.

How easily we can justify nearly anything in own minds. By rationalizing even the most unbelievable occurrences, we claim that *things happen*. We know uttering regretted words happens, and baseless thoughts manifest themselves in the human mind's darkest corners. Throughout our lives, we've seen ill-conceived thoughts and inflammatory words incite hurtful actions that caused reverberations, forever impacting lives in a negative manner.

If we're honest with ourselves, we'd probably prefer to exist in a constant state of peace whenever possible. Most agree living in harmony is preferable to drinking a bitter root (Deuteronomy 29:18), killing ourselves, crushing our heart and spirit, and ruining all the lives around us due to being hardheaded and allowing the odious to remain.

Forgiveness allows:
- All to thrive amidst times of great adversity in our world.
- Release from being stuck in unforgiving attitudes and ways.
- Freedom from obstacles that prevent living life fully.

Infertile soil to grow relationships is found in a life not based on truth. Whatever is lacking, the condition doesn't provide essentials for nurturing healthy, stable relationships. The resulting harvest may appear in many different ways. Unintentional health consequences develop from inflamed inner turmoil, spiritual burnout, and declining mental health. Attempts to artificially replace significant losses through immediate gratification by surrounding oneself with comfort can lead to financial woes, linked with an impaired view of the real world.

To fill a painful void, addiction or self-comforting is the side effect of a continual quest to ply ourselves only with what is pleasing. This insulating quest sedates us in living our life, shrouds the light of reality, and eventually results in a diminished legacy. Living a life based on truth offered in love is what God wants for us. It's a blessing how a simple concept challenges us to rise above the fray and resolve hard issues in such a profound way.

Forgiving is a win for everyone. When we release ourselves from the self-imposed inertia troubling issues have on us, we are freed to enjoy a full life. When we extend grace, we empower the forgiven to move forward. Through the act of forgiveness, everyone is freed from chains. This permits each to experience resolution on a matter and grow from there. Extending grace in truth and love releases all involved from the relational bondage.

The act of forgiving requires letting go of perceived control over an issue. It's impossible to carry a burdensome past and live forward fully. These burdens crowd out what matters most, allowing precious little time or accurate focus for living life. Instead of working toward restoration, we decline blessings by exalting our periphery in falsely believing it serves as a protective barrier from further suffering. We are insulated from restoration and sealed with a promise to drown in a dark swirl of personal vanity.

Getting out of our head and into our heart is the first step. When it is abundantly clear an unresolved issue is taking away from the fullness of life, the truth is evident. How will we move forward from this place, living free and traveling lighter? To see with the eyes of our heart is to see with perfect vision.

. . .

Where Forgiveness Comes From

A timeworn saying reminds us, "if you don't stand for something, you'll fall for anything." Having the strength of our convictions is a good thing, isn't it? Many are brought up to embrace this philosophy, living life based upon firmly held beliefs. We justify this fundamental driving force, knowing to live otherwise is building a presence on shifting sands.

What happens when we're drawn into a discussion with someone who disagrees with us? How does that go? How do we feel? Challenged? Maligned? What happens to that relationship? Does it survive and thrive? Does it fall apart under pressure?

What happens if someone says something offensive? What if we are personally threatened? What if someone banishes us from their life because we're inconvenient? How do we handle these situations?

What if someone steals something from us? Maybe we gave them the keys to our home or heart, and they took that trust as liberty to walk away with something they'd rather have than a relationship with us. What do we do?

Of course, I'm not suggesting Christian beliefs should change to fit the inconsistent worldview. Nothing is ever solved by rationalizing how and why unacceptable things occur or by diminishing the offense and personally absorbing a part of the blame for being in the way to receive the undeserved. Humans do stupid things, and so it has been since time began. History has proven this.

As Christians, we are called to follow Jesus' example by living a life based on truth offered in love. While it is impossible for mortals to replicate His innocent life in every way, our best attempts and innermost heart's desire to seek Him lights our path, even in the darkest of times.

Living in truth means we recognize undesirable things will happen. We are not promised an easy time in this life. The Bible reminds us difficulties are a certainty and provides instruction for dealing with them.

Living life in love means we must find forgiveness within

ourselves. Love and grace first come to us from God, then take residence within our heart. When we admit we are all imperfect beings, forgiveness offered in love to a wrongdoer is possible.

In John 13:34, Jesus said:
Let me give you a new command: Love one another. In the same way I loved you, you love one another.

By following Jesus Christ, His example and words, our way forward to forgiving is not as uncertain a task as our human mind would have us believe. We have no other choice. There is no better way. Stand for compassion for one another in love, grace, and peace.

Not Forgiving Creates a Self-inflicted Obstacle
Obstructing restoration of a broken relationship seems to be an easy solution whenever someone creates havoc, hurts us, or remaining connected becomes agonizing. What we don't realize at the time is we are erecting barriers to further complicate forgiving. We have taken a bold step to identify infractions, levied judgment on the person, and set parameters to keep them a safe distance from us.

This helps us contain a fractured relationship, giving us a sense that we can understand and control it. This futile action is a short-term way to acknowledge an infraction, calling it as we believe it to be, with unavoidable long-term consequences remaining.

Our condemnation might be based on personal observation or witnessing improper actions. Maybe our relationship has become tainted with a pervasive feeling about something we know nothing about but are inclined to believe. Whatever it appears to be, it hangs in the air, sucking the joy out of life. Based on fact or not, this has caused a break in the relationship that needs to be repaired.

No matter how dedicated our efforts, fully understanding every contributing factor surrounding a painful situation (or figuring all the convoluted nuances) isn't humanly possible. Trying to make sense of that which doesn't, only further confounds life. The Bible reminds us that in the church, as it is in relationships and spilling over into our everyday lives, "this is a huge mystery" (Ephesians 5:32a). So, let's not further encumber ourselves as we "pretend to understand it all," as Paul warns us in this passage. The way forward makes the growing need for restoration evident.

Always an unwelcome companion, unresolved issues will oppress every endeavor. Try as we may to avoid or deny, they remain steadfastly at our side. Eventually, it is clear this situation is holding us back. The truth is this will continue to distress us and negatively impact relationships until we banish it. This release occurs when issues are no longer given precedence over our lives, as we take necessary steps toward restoring relational breaks.

How we arrive at the place of making this change is when we come to the end of the road upon which we've been traveling. We can go no further. We either must turn around or strike out and blaze a new trail—but only if we are brave.

Upon reviewing a troubling matter, a shocking revelation occurs when we own the fact that our judgment of another (in part) fostered an environment to create this situation. Relationships involve more than one person. Even if a break wasn't initially caused by our personal choices or treating others badly, it was our reaction that created a greater divide in the crumbling relationship.

Recognizing involvement in a devastating personal matter can strike a tremendous blow with waves of pain ebbing and flowing throughout our body. This overriding sensation returns with every stark reminder. It becomes wearisome, filling our mind, weighing down our heart, tormenting us. After a while, it nags at us, calling out for attention. Every step, every breath becomes labored. Running and hiding are no longer feasible options (if they ever were). The ebb and flow of our pain can become the tide of change, bringing peace into our lives. We can discover this when we dare to step out in faith.

Immersed in a clash, how easy it is to fall into confusion and worry about a troubling situation. It's difficult to determine the right way to handle a problem when we suddenly realize we don't (necessarily) know everything about it. The earnest quest for seeking the best way to address it—to solve the problem and resolve the tension—soon replaces that jarring annoyance.

But how do we go about making this wronged thing right again? We've already experienced staggering discomfort and profound sadness of disconnect. No wonder we grow weary of how cumbersome life has become, littered with painful reminders. Sensing that we're missing something beautiful intended for us increases our pain and deepens regret.

Making the Most of the Journey

Our journey has been a long, winding path to arrive here today. Perhaps life is not as sweet as we once thought. In the deepest recesses of our heart, we admit it's possible we've missed some beautiful moments that we will never regain. We know we can't go back to where we never were, retrieving those things we've lost. But we can forge a new way to restoration, a fuller life, and a better future.

As we begin this trek, a guide to help us on this uncharted course is essential. The first step is to recognize no matter how we view a situation, we are not in charge—God is. The way forward is to pray about troubling issues and prayerfully consider the aching desires of our heart as we ask for the guidance and understanding only He can provide. His loving care is available to all who earnestly seek Him. It's wonderful how our heart and mind are reshaped and renewed. As we pray in this way, our mind gains greater clarity. Our perspective takes on a much broader view. Through this transformation, our steps become surer, and we know we have a reliable, trustworthy travel companion who always keeps His promises.

Looking at the matter with new eyes, we may understand that those with whom we've lost a relationship also need to experience the closeness of caring people, now more than ever. At no time did they need to have us slam the door in their face or cut off all contact. What if we were the only one who would have ever been able to help them? Emotions cause people to act, not logic. Emotions slam the door shut, but reasoning and understanding open it in truth and love.

In cases of rape or other abuse, victims should never risk their personal safety by attempting to contact their abuser or rekindle a relationship with their perpetrator to work toward forgiveness. A necessary step in these cases is looking at the situation with new eyes, identifying the wrong done, and seeing a way clear with a fresh start.

Forgiving doesn't mean we condone unacceptable behaviors, but through restoration, it permits the opportunity for us to influence others positively. It helps wrongdoers know a much better way to live (by example) while releasing us from the predicament. Think about it. If someone unexpectedly made an expressed effort to forgive you for something shameful you did, and speaking in truth told you how important you were in their lives, how would you feel?

Assurances will come in the days ahead on this journey. No matter what happened, it's never all about us, even if we somehow played a part in the unfolding drama. No matter what happened, it's all about relationship. We are not helpless or left alone to choose how to handle a situation. Our troubles are never too much for God, who stands with us. Pure faith allows us to rest in Christ in all matters throughout our days. Remembering the judgment seat is not man's property rightfully acknowledges God's unchanging scriptural precepts we live by. Going our own way will never lift a heavy burden from our heart.

Knowing we are not the first to experience these afflictions gives us a sense of belonging. Accepting the fact we cannot fix everything on our own (or we would) allows us opportunity to rely on Jesus every step of our way. We are drawn closer to Him, deeper into our intended life. Never alone, we can live a grace-filled life, surrounded by love.

. . .

Mistaken Forgiveness

I once heard someone's description of forgiveness as a stooping down to extend grace to a wrongdoer. Through my research, writing, and ongoing conversations on this topic, I've concluded this definition is about 50 percent correct in principle. The problem with this statement is the posturing is wrong.

Understanding what forgiveness is *not*, is as important as knowing what forgiveness *is*. Not having a clear grasp of the concept of how we extend grace will result in futile efforts to make amends.

Restoring relationships is challenging when navigation on the road to grace is littered with potential misfires and undesirable landmines caused by relying on old mindsets and unreliable common practices. Need proof? If these established practices and beliefs worked, this book would be unnecessary.

Why make such a daunting endeavor more difficult? Hitting the mark is key to moving forward in relational restoration. If we are going to take action to mend a broken relationship, every step counts. Getting it right is essential, or else we continue to fan the flames of discourse.

A crystal-clear frame of reference for this noble act provides the needed stability to start out on the right foot. We can't predict how our best efforts will play out, but we can pray. Knowing what forgiveness is not is a great place to start.

Gracing someone with forgiveness is not proving who was right (after all) in a troubling matter. Not now, not after many years of a broken relationship, or not even one dying an agonizingly slow death in plain sight.

No one can rightfully claim a win in achieving the forgiveness process. Correctly accomplished, it is something to celebrate. No one in a relationship is the designated peacemaker because accomplishing restoration takes all parties involved to move forward in this effort.

Forgiving another never serves as evidence of someone's unmatched superiority or immeasurable benevolence. With a right heart, one's desire to make things right is apparent in an otherwise unacceptable situation.

Making things right for abuse and rape victims means holding the perpetrator accountable for their actions while releasing all parties through prayer, made possible only by the grace and strength God provides.

So, what is this elusive thing we call forgiveness? It is a move toward restoring a damaged relationship initiated by one flawed individual to another, by extending grace. No stooping down is needed, as we are in this together.

In writing this book, I discovered some commonly employed techniques in relational matters. See if you've observed any of these yourself:

- **The Holding Pattern** is an intended relational pause mode that causes a delay in action for an undetermined situation to occur or develop, related to a particular matter. The person who pushed this button doesn't necessarily know what the wait is about because the next step is unclear. Waiting at this place seems better than nothing.
- **Nonsensical Justification** is a valiant attempt to make sense of something that doesn't make sense. In all earnestness, we would exonerate, if we could. If accomplishing this were possible, then everything would be alright as we earnestly apply this situational bandage that never really sticks.
- **Hands-free Forgiveness** is a convenient approach, universally acceptable in these dizzying days of automation. Granting blessings and grace freely to others intuitively in an autopilot kind of way, blankets intended recipients, auto-magically dispensing the grace granter's implied affirmation with the hope the message is received.
- **Deep-dive Thinking** (also known as over-thinking) is trying to comprehend everything surrounding a matter. It requires placing each element extracted from a troubling situation under a relational microscope, carefully examining the why, when, who, and how of it.

Once all components are reviewed and tested, we can move on to forgiveness. As with all research, this can take an inordinate amount of time. Unfortunately, the final results may be incorrect or inconclusive because all the facts cannot be gathered.

Why do we tend to make things more difficult than they need to be? Why do we add insurmountable obstructions to an already daunting situation? Applying any of the above methods (and others) permits an already painful condition to linger and fester. It is obvious we get in our way of moving toward resolution of an uncomfortable matter.

These ineffective actions hinge on the basic human need for authority and control in life, especially over all matters that personally involve us. It becomes a control issue when we place ourselves at the epicenter of any vexing situation. To be fair, it is possible we did not deserve some of the hurtful things that happened to us. Under these circumstances, it seems the only way to deal with these matters is to take charge of them in the best way possible.

Unfortunately, taking the commander's seat of a painful predicament does not promise to make everything better. This approach only gives those who desire control a false sense of being in charge of the known uncontrollable factors, arming them with the hope of stemming any additional flow of personal distress or embarrassment. As followers of Christ, we already know the judgment seat is taken, and it is not ours.

Some People Seem Easier to Forgive

It's ironic that we can feel an incredible kinship with those not related to us in any way, while not having a true understanding of how that feels with our own family. If this is the case, is this shared affinity an idealized feeling? This makes us wonder if the relationship is sustainable.

Depending upon our personal circumstances—along with the

depth and quality of our relationships—seemingly endless grace may be lavished to the extent of willful blindness to reality. This marvelous safety net of adoring friends, family, and colleagues may stick with us no matter what comes next, or we may discover the bleak severity of being completely alone, at the brink of facing our biggest crisis. It comes most unexpectedly. Even after years of personal support, near daily attention, gifts, and loving care, at our time of greatest need, these friends are nowhere to be seen.

This jarring awareness is a real-life wake-up call. Yesterday's friends with today's disappearing act are gone. It doesn't necessarily mean they weren't sincere or never cared. It's simply their way of letting you know they can go no further with you on this part of your journey. They have their reasons. It may be too arduous for them to face this with you, probably because they don't have that deeply wired default connection inherently born into a family. As close as we are (or at one time were), this doesn't exist.

Family dynamics differ. Some will try to deny the fact of being wired for connection, but look at those certain family ways, resemblances, and similarities carried into future generations. Interestingly enough, upon returning to the fold, seeking those who've known us longest and best, we may discover they await our return (like the prodigal) at the moment they needed restoration most.

Except in situations posing personal safety concerns, we have no right to not remain in relationship with one another. Whether family or friend, we all need each other in this world. Some cannot give as much to a relationship as others, but all have gifts to share and needs we can address in our own way. We grow and learn through relationships. As they develop, we hope to feel connected and closer. This feeling is part of the essential foundation of a life lived in love.

God gave us our families, those who took us in as their own, to bless us. Through relational difficulties and life challenges, we are offered the possibility to understand forgiveness better. We have opportunities to discover the shared human need of extending grace to live at peace with one another.

When we embrace speaking truth in love (through prayer) to change lives, restoration begins. God is masterful at mending hurting hearts and setting things right.

The book of Job recounts Job's restoration after he lost his family, his wealth, and his health. But despite his stunning losses, he remained faithful to God throughout his suffering. By questioning God, Job grew in his understanding of God's sovereignty. Knowing he couldn't do anything on his own to fix his situation, he knew he needed to trust the Lord.

An example of the power of prayer in healing and restoration amidst the chaos is found in Job 42:10. In this passage, God called Job to pray for his friends after they slandered him and God. Job prayed as instructed. God answered his prayers by restoring Job's life in ways far exceeding the great prosperity and joy of his earlier life.

Like Job, when we pray for others who hurt us (not praying for our own personal gain), we will receive unexpected results in the form of unimaginable blessings. God faithfully answers our prayers when we pray for the needs of others and for their provision. In the process, He blesses us in incredible ways. When we seek Him in our life storms, He will comfort us and help us through.

We will never be able understand the whys behind suffering. Bad things happen to good people. Righteous people suffer. Innocents are victimized. All suffering cannot be blamed on the sufferer's life. As God delivers believers from torment, the wrongdoers will most assuredly receive their punishment from Him.

Living a life of faith requires endurance to continue running this race, coupled with perseverance to finish it. As Job told his wife, believers don't live on *Easy Street*. They must accept both the good and the troubles in life (Job 2:10). We can rest in God's sovereignty as Job did. Through it all, God remains near us and is able to help us out of our plight. He will surely deliver all suffering believers either in this life or in the eternal life to come (Isaiah 54:17).

. . .

Through Wrong Eyes, Seeing is Deceiving

"Seeing is believing" is the world's timeworn philosophy and practice. This mindset runs contrary to the Christian practice of walking by faith and not by sight (2 Corinthians 5:7). Too many Christians straddle the fence by ascribing to both traditions. Perhaps in this way, they hedge their aim, hoping to hit the mark more accurately. Indeed, nearly all strive in some way to understand, even if our means differ.

Life flows better when we assume people are doing their best. Living with this perspective removes us from a place of judgment. We're not compelled to interject our ideas of how to do things nor contemplate how things could otherwise be. These activities slow our pace, hampering relationships.

By focusing on our personally established priorities, we can see things for what they are, not as we perceive (or wish) them to be. In the process, we may be able to nurture close bonds with those who are important in our lives.

Unfortunately, *seeing* can be deceiving. Have you ever noticed what someone did or heard what they said, and you're sure you know there's something more behind the scenes they're not sharing? Or another person's reactions or conversation (maybe their lack of communication) causes you to think there's something they're not telling you? An element of judgment inevitably slips into the picture as we attempt to draw a concrete conclusion as something to hold onto at each juncture.

All relationships involve real people and caring hearts. A true connection with another may require limited personal involvement but provide an essential tie to the everyday. People are not synthetic. At the core of our humanness, we will perceive, do, and believe as we authentically are. As our paths cross, a caring heart at the receiving end makes our connection complete.

A caring heart sees deeper. It hears and knows every nuance in a relationship. It never second-guesses. If allowed, it can sense all the hills and valleys, knows every winding trail and rocky crag. It doesn't need directions or a GPS to get there because it recognizes the way, even to places it has never been.

Isn't it a fascinating realization when we tell someone we completely understand as they share their heart with us, even while we have never personally experienced what they described? We are *there* with them.

The view is always clearest when you see through the caring eyes of your heart. It is in this place where relationships are nurtured, restored, and grown. A caring heart is a place where you will see things as they are, with a pure light of love cast on people. Heart-to-heart is how you will come to better understand their hopes, dreams, and fears.

As we explore the concept of forgiveness further, its simplicity will be illustrated. A clear understanding of forgiveness removes unnecessary barriers. This allows us to move forward more confidently. When our heart's desire becomes focused on taking steps toward restoring broken relationships, we're much closer to making amends with others, and restoration becomes possible.

Forgiving in Real Life: Apply the Principles and Live these Truths by Prayerful Consideration

Do you have a troubling matter weighing heavy on your heart?

Are you able to identify what is holding you back from repairing it?

Are you willing to begin to work toward restoration?

Grace gives meaning to life. It tells us what is right and what is not. It reminds us that when we've done wrong, we can make a situation right through forgiveness.

Grace is favor extended freely without expectation, payment, discussion, or recompense. It restores the brokenness so we can move on.

When grace is given, forgiveness happens. Forgiveness shows us someone undeniably loves us enough to hold us closer still.

Action steps

Prayerfully explore how to move forward, seeking God's guidance.

Consider each step a reset of what was—progress toward restoration.

Record what you know about the issue and any insight you gain in your reading, study, and prayer about forgiveness in your journal.

SEVEN
DON'T WANT TO FORGIVE

Consider the Cost of Not Forgiving

There is a cost to everything in life. We are always subject to a direct cost for doing things, as well as for failed attempts. For every choice we make (good or bad), there is an expense incurred. The charge assessed for things done, and for things left undone, is inescapable. We pay the cost of our choices through the life consequences we experience.

As we are busy living our lives, we don't take adequate time to consider our actions (reactionary knee-jerks) in our daily interactions. Ill-chosen words exchanged in passing create a chill in the air. Searing words fired-off in the heat of a passionate moment leave a scar. Inaction on our part by refusing to aid another creates a void of indifference.

While the effect of our carelessness may seem to be laid on those we ply with a lack of regard, our life is impacted in ways not yet fully calculated. Most assuredly, the charges will eventually come to us with a high balance to be paid. In some instances, the cost is a priceless loss we can never regain. Once figured, a shocking realization sets in that there will be no recovery as these losses transform into a bleak forfeiture of what we could have experienced in enjoying life's blessings.

It's All About Relationship

If we're honest, we know we're better together, even with differences. God hardwired us for connection, and we are naturally drawn into a community to share, for mutual support and affirmation. This is our God-given human nature.

Teams are a form of community. If nurtured, marital bonds can form into a kind of team. In the early days of my own marriage, it didn't take my husband and me long to realize two unified heads were usually better than one in most decision-making situations. A group of friends or family may serve as informal teams in our lives. Special interest groups or other organizations like our church may also be a team.

How team members interact amongst themselves—and our connection with them—directly affects our lives in unimaginable ways. Personal choices and the way we may live life, are in some ways impacted by those within our sphere of influence.

Our teams may be supportive of us, or not. Our interaction with them flavors our relationship:

- How do we treat the friend we love who doesn't ever have time to get together with us?
- What are our interactions like with church family members whose worship music and service style preferences differ from ours?
- What about a straying family member we say we understand? Are we simply enabling their behavior with no concern from us?
- How do we encourage ministering to others as we continue to serve those in need who express disappointment for whatever we give them?

. . .

Life Losses are Irreplaceable

No matter what our role is, or the association we have with others, if someone simply crosses paths with us or serves on one of our teams, lives are impacted.

Think of the lives Jesus touched as He encountered the hurting and lost through His ministry of miracles (Matthew 8:1-9:34):

- Jesus healed the man with leprosy. (Matthew 8:1-4)
- Jesus healed the centurion's servant. (Matthew 8: 5-13)
- Jesus healed Peter's mother-in-law. (Matthew 8:14-17)
- Jesus calmed the storm on the lake. (Matthew 8: 23-27)
- Jesus restored two demon-possessed men. (Matthew 8: 28-34)
- Jesus healed a paralytic. (Matthew 9:1-8)
- Jesus brought a ruler's daughter back to life. (Matthew 9:18-26)
- Jesus healed two blind men. (Matthew 9:27-31)
- Jesus healed a mute, demon-possessed man. (Matthew 9:32-33)

What if Jesus felt too busy to deal with a problem or decided to put off healing someone until another time? What if one day Jesus decided to withhold healing someone because He chose to turn the helpless and harassed away? What if He chose to take a personal day off from His important work?

If none of these miracles occurred, the lives He touched would have been left untreated. If Jesus decided He was not going to follow God's plan for His life to die on the cross for the forgiveness of our sins (John 3:16-18), what hope or salvation could we ever claim? He obediently followed His Father's plan and stayed true to His earthly mission of salvation for all (Luke 19:1-10).

Our loving heavenly Father sent His only son not only to die for our salvation but to serve as an example of how to live an extraordinary life. This doesn't mean we make miracles happen, but it does mean when we love through life's hard places and touch hurting hearts, amazing things can happen. Make no mistake about it; nails did not hold Jesus on the cross. It was intentional love.

Correctly applied, discernment plays a part in forgiving. A wrong must first be identified, followed by the admitted need to pardon. Feelings and emotions easily come into play.

Like shifting sands, these elements never provide a solid foundation upon which to base a sound decision. Inaccurate discernment gives way to reactionary behavior. Our approach can compound or allay a festering situation.

Choices and decisions are uniquely shaped by an individual's personal selective perception. Actions and reactions occur based on how people see things. Maybe a view is shaped by a whim of this moment. As fickle as we humans are, our perception varies greatly from one another. We don't typically agree squarely on all matters with others, do we?

Here are a few conditions that can alter how viewing things affect our relationships:

- **Circumstances**

Our relationships are affected by how others view us. This includes how we live. Even a failing memory can remember how others treated them as the person they were perceived to be. Our perspective, how we are addressed (and treated), the extent and true depth of our relationships and personal associations ultimately depend upon several factors: background, beliefs, desires (shape interaction), discernment, and willingness to forgive.

For instance, people will treat a known convicted criminal entirely different from a high school honor student. Granted, they may be years apart in age, but their station in life, how they present themselves, and how they are regarded by their accomplishments, affects all relationships with others.

If a convicted criminal did his time and is released back into society, he carries an officially documented accounting of recognized wrongs with him. Because his record is a public matter, there is no hiding it. Once identified, this person is automatically viewed in a different light and regarded differently by most members of any community.

Some may forgive freely, recognizing this person has made reparation and is now beginning anew. Those distrustful of the criminal justice system will always believe this person was wrongfully accused, feeling pity for most prisoners. Aware of past wrongs, others may still hold this person at a distance, never trusting. Fearful or uncertain, others may do everything they can to remain in this person's good graces at all times. Each is a different reaction to the same person and set of circumstances, influenced by every individual's set of beliefs and personal experiences.

It may stun us to face the similarities between extending grace to a convicted criminal who has served their sentence and an everyday individual called out as having caused what is widely viewed as an unforgivable incident.

Recognizing circumstantial scope, scale, and degree of inflicted damage varies. Nonetheless, a wrong has been done, accounted for, and punishment applied. Except in cases of personal safety, the next step is to issue a personal pardon to build a relationship on the rubble, with the promise of a new beginning.

As individuals work through troubling situations, they acknowledge an affront and consider their perpetrator in an attempt to understand everything surrounding the event. Discernment will determine what to do about it. Will it be forgiven? Shall we forget about it? Can it be overlooked? When can we move forward? Is it better to ignore everything related to it?

How a problem (and perpetrator) is viewed and handled is fashioned by everyone's unique perspective. This practice is never as effective (or final) as God's loving manner of covering all with his blanket of grace.

. . .

- **Mindset**

The offender may never be in a place to accept a victim's extended forgiveness or grace. Once caught, a perpetrator may even go to the extent of denying any need for a pardon. Willingly refusing to acknowledge a troubling matter makes restoration more uncertain.

The wronged may never face their perpetrator personally, especially in cases risking personal safety. None of these situations will cease the ability to extend absolution to a wrongdoer. Mindset, perspective, and thoughts significantly impact each individual, affecting resolve.

If the instigator believes no wrong has been done and holds an air of entitlement, denying credence to claims made, they have ensconced themselves in a space where they feel most comfortable. The evildoer believes this position is deemed as a safe place offering sheltered superiority, with an excellent vantage point for showing greater strength. It might seem so for a while, but the truth never remains hidden for long.

Those who have been hurt may feel forgotten, helpless, and reduced to exist in excruciating pain for what seems like an eternity. It all becomes more unbearable when outsiders interject personal perceptions about an incident. This may occur by victim-blaming, rationalizing bad things out loud, and trying to make sense of things that never will. Some prefer to remain at a safe distance instead of displaying an apparent lack of empathy in considering something causing another discomfort.

Bystanders can't imagine such a thing occurring. They may even know both parties involved, possibly favoring one over the other. Maybe they're rooting for the wrong actor. When true wickedness is unleashed, most are blindsided. No one's mind could ever have imagined such a thing. They are left speechless. Some may think they're just glad it wasn't them, while remaining helpless to find appropriate comforting words for the victim.

Taking a step forward seems perilous. Perception affects actions —taken or not. The mindset of those involved can positively affect the resolution of the unimaginable. Holding firm standards as a personal foundation provides a solid operational base.

Life is filled with the unexpected. Reactionary fear may be a human trait, but it is not part of living a faith-based life. Action is required. When faced with a menacing threat or nestled in the smoldering ashes of the aftermath, knowing what you stand for provides guidance for charting a course through turbulent waters.

Time and distance prepare the way for effectively working through adversity. Seeking God's guidance and protection through prayer, He will provide needed understanding. Following His ways always assures appropriate actions.

• **Needs**

Everyone shares the basic human needs for survival: food, shelter, and nurturing. Some requirements are stronger than others. Some become a driving force to be filled. Sometimes we incorrectly consider our desires as needs.

Life can easily skew off into unintended directions in a confused mash-up of needs, desires, goals, and dreams. If we're not careful, they will become intermingled. Lacking clarity, each may be given the same weight of importance, blending all of them together to form a tangled mess.

Human desires, perceived personal needs, and preferences shape our interactions and relationships with others. It's not just how we view a situation or someone, but what we hope to receive as a result of our connection. Personal priorities and beliefs impact our ability to build and maintain relationships—or not.

For instance, most people do care what others think of them, because a public image is still an essential key to many things hoped for at work, at school, and in life. Because it is important to have civil discourse, authentic opinions or thoughts may not be openly shared with a casual acquaintance, a professor, coworker, or others. Some beliefs and feelings may be forever locked away, deep within a person's heart. White lies are told to hide the hurtful truth or serve as camouflage for strong opinions.

For many, a deep-seated fear that others will think less of them due to diverging viewpoints can result in word parsing and modifying actions in ways other than intended. Creating a soft, cushiony insulation for personal safety doesn't allow someone to get too close to the real person behind a carefully crafted public façade.

Political correctness provides anyone seeking a safe place a publicly recognized curtain to hide behind. It effectively directs conversation about things never to be discussed and ideas never to be shared. Think of the difference it could make to step out and courageously speak the truth.

• Heart Condition

How we regard others, and our relationship with them, affects all aspects of life. We may never have met a stranger, seemingly having endless friends and acquaintances always glad to see our smiling face. Maybe our sphere of influence is small but comprised of a close-knit group of caring friends and family where authentic love and dedication run deep.

While connecting points are different, heart condition is similar in both cases. Each encourages relationship. Perfect harmony with friends, family, and acquaintances isn't possible. Remaining available to those around them, caring for the important people in their lives in a shared relationship is a great joy. Because personal relationships are top priority, they remain dedicated to their people. We can too.

Being human, a misstep or misunderstanding is inevitable. Even with a heart that wants to live life in an open, understanding, forgiving way, talking about uncomfortable moments with others can still be difficult. Honestly making an attempt to reconnect with the hope of repairing the break in a relationship is a step toward mending the tear.

No matter how large or small the gap, a person with an open

heart wants to make the situation right as quickly as possible. It's how they roll. It's how they live life. They live more freely, unencumbered by heavy burdens. Their minds are clear of problems controlling their lives. As much as possible, they have made an attempt to live at peace and in harmony with those around them.

We cannot control all things, but we can control our own reactions to the unexpected or ill treatment. No matter the circumstances, we choose how to live. In the process of developing a kind of resiliency, we grow into the kind of experience and heart we have.

To those whom much is given, much is also expected in return (Luke 12:48). Grace and freedom are generously granted. When we know the joy and how beautiful it is to live a life on-course, we must bless others by encouraging them to live their best life as well. When those challenging times require our attention, we should be gracious to others. Because we are unique individuals, our life experiences differ significantly from each other, but basic foundational principles remain the same. As humans, we all have a heart. How have you set the course of your heart?

• Artists of Misdirection

In the gravity of an impromptu moment fueled by fear of impending negative consequences, some will portray themselves as victim of an incident they participated in. Maybe they fear how it would look to others if their involvement was known, so they go out of their way to demonstrate how they were not involved. This campaign may hold credibility for a while but will not stand the test of time.

This strategy can work at least for a while when artists of misdirection have a healthy support system comprised of related parties who could also be impacted if such a transgression became public knowledge. In such cases, great care is taken to effectively apply camouflage. Tracks are covered. Highly orchestrated subterfuge begins.

The stage is set to make any report by the oppressed perceived as not credible. It is an impossible uphill battle, far beyond the he-said-she-said technique. If all participants play, it turns into a strategic game of viciousness. The initial set-up is established far enough in advance so that making a move to counter the charges becomes nearly impossible.

Sometimes the storyteller is one who cannot face the truth. Losing the beautiful girlfriend isn't the end of their story, but it is an indicator of a potential inability to maintain a relationship, to part amicably, or make a clean break.

Alcoholism or addiction will often take precedence in life, creating a lack of drive or ambition to make a better way in the world. In these situations, the partner takes the fall since the one left behind will not accept personal responsibility for either moving forward or for any significant loss.

Time never serves as a soothing salve in a life of restlessness or unrealized potential. Considering all the negative traits of that wretched woman—how wrong was willfully done; how the employer had it in for the lowly worker—venomous feelings are further inflamed, increased with each telling.

Through years of recounting a sordid tale, details become firebrands that scar the teller's heart. Since the situation was apparently out of the self-proclaimed victim's control, in their mind this is the only way to make things right. By casting the other party in an unfavorable light, they believe they can receive justification but remain trapped with what they most abhor.

In the process, their agony plays out in an endless loop. Their suffering ensnares them. They remain stuck, hopelessly languishing in the land of unresolved consequences, forever sentenced to live trapped in a sticky web of invisible limbo, with no foreseeable escape. There is no way out of this hellish nightmare.

In some cases, misrepresentations may develop into an all-out act of war that lasts for years. As each opportunity arises, yet another volley is executed by the coward in an attempt to wear the scapegoat down further so they will not try to speak their truth, nor remain to present their case rightfully against this dominant, warring faction. The main point is to dig a trench deep enough for protection, while warding off the anticipated enemy fire, which would allow the facts to be revealed.

• Fear Factor

People fear what they don't understand. They will go to great lengths to ward off an unwelcome encounter. Previously unimagined measures may be taken with the unexpressed purpose to avoid dealing with it at nearly any cost. Intentionally denying an incident is a shortsighted strategy. It's based on ground rules that, like an invisible intruder, make it hard to address that which you fail to recognize (or see) exists. Instant justification is granted for any action the willing participant takes when playing this mind game.

Unfortunately, this is not a successful play because the hurt remains. Wishing to avoid a reality they had hoped never to know, they find themselves in a weakened position. Their pain intensifies with the discovery that they've allowed themselves to be played for a sucker by someone playing fast and loose. Someone with the mindset to win will be victorious in this round no matter what.

This leads to another favorite, equally ineffective approach: an attempt to destroy that which isn't understood. Now, all-out efforts are suddenly in play. The gun is reloaded, and any moving target will be fired upon. Total desecration is the goal (Romans 12:1).

Flames of resentment, anger, and rage can easily be fanned into an enormous conflagration of revenge by anyone who has this vicious spark in their heart. Once set, the fire rages wildly, rapidly engulfing everything as far as the human eye can see. The once lush landscape is devastated, and the playing surface is now leveled. In the end, it seems all that comprised life has been completely eviscerated.

In reality, this is as far as the human eye wants to see. The hurting heart may be too weary, and the victor too sure of the vast extent of intended demise unleashed, to be able to see things as they really are.

The fiery revenge did accomplish moving forgiveness further out of immediate grasp but not out of the realm of possibility. Hatred and bitterness will do that on any given day. However, as it has been since the beginning of time on this earth, hope always arises out of the ashes of any fire. Hope is always found there. It awaits discovery.

• Fear of Being Discovered

A fascinating (and unexpected) chain of events sometimes blazes a new trail that uncovers the truth through revealing a surprising discovery. This is what those with hidden addictions, adulterers, thieves, bullies, chronic liars, abusers, and other perpetrators who prefer to hide in darkness fear the most. Once found out, there is no hiding the truth. Eventually, something is going to occur, causing an undesirable change in their preferred method of daily operation.

The curious thing is the truth eventually (in most cases) makes itself apparent. Thankfully, it usually needs no help. Despite the most dedicated efforts to hide related evidence, talented character acting and mock pretension in mounting a grand persuasive campaign of self-promotion, those human efforts turn to dust over time.

Time may not be a healing agent, but it is an accurate indicator of what is fact. The truth may remain obscured for a while, but the cover eventually falls away, and the provocateur and their evil intent will be known by all eyes willing to see and hearts ready to believe the truth. Struck by the shocking nature of it all, thinking minds begin to know what the truth is, and it makes sense. Misrepresentation, cover-ups, and coordinated lies suddenly become evident.

Today's simple truth is anyone looking for an insult or to claim injury resulting from personal mistreatment is quickly served. An essential element in successful living is a clear understanding that interaction is all about a relationship involving others not based only on self-focus. We can convince ourselves of almost anything. Like lying to ourselves. We turn any truth upside down (in our favor), claiming it to be real. In this way, we can create our own world, placing our all-knowing selves at the center of our universe.

Disparate scenarios swirl about all of us. Every scene is as varied as the players. Sometimes camouflaged to fit neatly into our everyday life, they exist silently tucked away as a part of our surroundings. Another nagging problem may arise and cause quite a stir. It seems issues blow-up at the most inconvenient time. All have far-reaching ripple effects in the lives they touch.

Many who exist in this skewed netherworld deal with vexing issues, causing everyone to wonder how they got there:

- Dramatically played out on the stage of life and death, an emaciated teen believes she will never be thin enough.
- Convinced he will never be good enough, a sensitive, intelligent, young man believes all the bad things his father told him about himself, so he gives up trying.
- A drop-dead-gorgeous woman believes she is not beautiful or worthy and continues to seek approval.
- An esteemed pillar of the community has a wandering eye and lives with a conflicted heart between right and wrong.
- A misguided young lady believes if she cuts herself enough times, her pain will ease.
- Drug and alcohol addiction lead many down a dark path in futile attempts to build a secure place to hide from unceasing hurt. Their agony is accompanied by a string of their perceived personal failures, digging an even deeper pit into the darkness. It's just easier to give up. The future is hopeless.
- A husband serves his wife stale morsels of caring, never enough to nourish and sustain a relationship. Hungrily, she accepts far less than she's entitled to, settling for less, being publicly disrespected.

Forgiveness, love, and acceptance go a long way in healing life's pain.

. . .

What if Tomorrow Never Comes?

Withholding needed attention or a simple, caring word is not living Jesus' example. This is an intentional choice shaped by our selfish humanness. By honoring our own personal importance more than the essential life-breathing ways of our Lord, we prefer to take a chance by waiting for the moment we pick to make things right again, thinking it will be optimal for us. In doing so, we entirely disregard others and fail to consider the impact we have in a real relationship with them. The relationship still exists. It remains either restored or broken.

Consider these situations:
- The last word you spoke to a close friend or family member was when you were not at your best. You reassure yourself they know you well, and you really didn't mean it as it sounded.
- You have grave concern for someone you know is having difficulty. Permitting it to go on unchecked by not expressing your care and concern for them enables the painful situation. We can never change the person, but through words spoken in love for them, we can encourage the person to change.
- A matter has been laid on your heart to speak with a member of your church family. You see them every week. Forgetting to mention it this week, you convince yourself you'll remember next time. Will you remember? Will you even see them?

In choosing to withhold life-giving words and much-needed loving encouragement, we put ourselves first as we second-guess the future.

Letting critical moments that need restoration slip between our fingers assures us of carrying unwanted burdens forever. As we control what we choose to do, we can also be intentional about cleaning up our messes as they occur.

If you find yourself in a one-sided relationship that leaves you feeling hopeless, it doesn't take long to grow weary of wearing the I'm-not-your-personal-piñata badge, does it? The truth is it's never right to not forgive. If we are to live our lives as exampled by Jesus, forgiving is not an option or a personal choice.

Forgiving in Real Life: Apply the Principles and Live these Truths by Personal Challenge

Make a list of the various teams you have in your life.

Consider ways you are influenced by the members of these teams (positively or negatively).

What is your role or impact within each of these groups?

Action steps

Do any relationships come to mind that you should attend to? How will you address the matter?

Don't put it off. Put this book down and find a way to reach them—now!

EIGHT
UNFORGIVING SPIRITS

What Causes an Unforgiving Spirit?

Human nature provides fertile ground for developing a unique spin on what relationship means to us. Encounters requiring forgiveness are shaped by how we view and value relationships. This impacts how we treat others.

Emotions stirred by issues within a relationship influence how we deal with matters needing grace with that person. Personal perspective on what happened guides us in how we regard and address issues. In this way, our daily grace challenge is influenced by circumstances and situations that compel us to forgive freely—or not.

If we're honest, this is why most of us frequently fail to forgive others and ourselves. Our focus is wrong. Our desire to address a troubling situation is diminished by our perceived enormity (or triviality) of its importance.

In the moment, it's challenging to grasp that blame or hateful speech from others has little to do with the maligning individual when we are the unfortunate target of a grudge or find ourselves in a smear campaign. But wait for a moment. Hit pause on all the noise. Now, listen carefully. Removed from all the confusion, hear the words proclaimed, and you will know they speak volumes about the source of the rants.

Stepping back from a painful moment allows us to see with refreshed eyes and to hear with attentive ears. Within that protective space, we can discern that the spouted maliciousness isn't personal. It's not about us. But because we're drawn in, it feels like it is.

The Bible cautions us as believers to guard our heart because everything we do flows from there (Proverbs 4:23). Sometimes we find ourselves in awkward situations or things don't happen as we think they should. Events like these can easily result in an unforgiving spirit, despite our best intentions.

Here are some examples of how an unforgiving spirit can negatively affect lives:

- A child is repeatedly reminded he is not good enough, no matter what he does. Hoping to gain favor with his parents, the child determines to work harder. But no matter how relentless the child's attempts are to win his parents' attention, he remains nearly invisible to them. Regardless of how outstanding the public recognitions are for the child, no achievement is ever acknowledged by the parents. With each success, the goal posts are perpetually relocated a little further down the endless playing field, always just out of reach. In the end, the child never receives the one thing in life most desired—to hear his parents say they were proud of all his accomplishments. Was all the hard work and endless efforts worth it?

- After almost thirty years of marriage and growing a family, a spouse declares irreconcilable differences. The children are now young adults, successfully making their way in the world. A new chapter in the family's journey was about to begin, but this story takes a most unexpected twist. It hits a dead end. Perceived voids angrily cry out, demanding to be filled in new ways. Long-held regrets surface, perhaps sprouting from past sacrifices made and tireless dedication never fully appreciated. Unrealized lifelong desires hungrily gnaw at nearly empty hearts that can only be replenished with what is perceived as lacking.

- A young child's parent is murdered, forever robbing her of any relationship and positive influence in her life. The great loss compounds as the child grows up. In careful observation of other families, life somehow never seems as full as those children who have lived with both parents. The child (now an adult) is left only with dimming memories of the lost parent looked up to by one so young. Sadly, only idealistic images of what could have been are remnants. Life can never be as great as it could have been.

- A spouse with a hot temper takes frustrations out on the family. Regardless of the situation, it's always someone else's fault. Usually, the person receiving the misdirected anger has nothing to do with the offending incident and can't rectify it. They are repeatedly in the wrong place at precisely the right time to receive verbal abuse, serving as a scapegoat. Sometimes the aggressor addresses the matter but usually not. Venting repeatedly occurs and searing wrath is expressed, burying the hopeless family in a deep sadness.

Walking the Tightrope

Do you ever try to understand why things happened as they did? I know I have. The desire to interpret the pivotal events in our lives is wired into in our nature. This is a natural inclination for our survival in determining dangers to avoid. We can easily waste an inordinate amount of time trying to solve life's many unexplainable (and illogical) mysteries.

Examining relational motives is reliably inaccurate because we view things from our perspective without knowing all the facts. Before studying forgiveness so deeply, I'd never seen the inherent dangers in engaging in this futile exercise until I discovered how diametrically opposed this is to how believers should live.

We can never know everything. What if we're wrong? We could live an entire lifetime based solely on our own warped version of the truth. We don't know what we don't know, but living this way promises we will miss a lifetime of untold joys and beautiful moments. I've known people who lived like this. Have you?

When we try to make sense of hurtful things that happen, we embrace the world's practice of seeing is believing rather than living by faith and love. Christ-followers are called to trust what the eye cannot see but the heart can know.

We risk everything by placing ourselves in a higher position than humanly possible as all-knowing and inexhaustibly wise. This is mankind's prideful folly at its best.

Hurtful things never spring from loving motivation. The Bible tells us living with compassion and embracing truth is the right way to live. Remembering who we are as God's people, we can rest knowing He wants the best for us and always keeps His promises. If we let Jesus' light of truth shine through our lives like a beacon in the darkness, it will beckon all to a safer place. He lights even our darkest path.

While in the throes of adversity, it is difficult to attribute hateful messages heard, false things mistakenly perceived as truth, and difficulties endured as situations used by the Enemy with intent to rob us of all joy. Each scenario promises to separate us from those dear to us and threatens to diminish our relationship with our loving Lord.

If we choose to participate in matters that assail our spirit, we risk not only missing out on blessings intended for us, but potentially never living our life's purpose. How tragic to exist in constant turmoil that could be addressed. Allowing painful issues to dominate and direct life turns our focus away from experiencing God's best.

We must hold fast to what is true. God's promises will be fulfilled in His time. Living out His promises becomes our legacy. How we choose to live—forgiven, forgiving or not—will influence lives today, as well as those yet to be born.

How We See Things Shapes Our Forgiving Spirit

We may act on our personal blend of deduced information and render an assessment of a situation, never realizing we're going out on a limb because we lack facts. When acting as our rational selves, we contemplate some motivation or driving force possibly based on a fragment of truth. While we may never be able to explain or understand why something happened, we know for sure hurtful things never spring from loving motivation.

Have you ever noticed people will stop everything to be taken in by what they perceive as a compelling story? Our curious nature enables us to be captivated when our attention is grabbed by an intriguing message. It's easy to be swept away as we listen, potentially giving credence to doublespeak pronouncements like an exclusive insider's scoop. Adding this fuel to the fire encourages inflammatory telling of more tales.

To catch a glimpse of a potential inferno, think back to some he-said-she-said events. This is a dangerous place that promises great risk of getting mired in a sticky tangle. It grows increasingly difficult to escape with every twist. If not resolved, the intended prey (and others joining the fray) may be trapped. They remain held there, kept from fully living life. It may have begun with just a simple story.

From my observations, people who listen most intently to these tall tales are not personally involved. They are merely intrigued bystanders looking for an entertaining train wreck. If they believe the untruths that are fed to them, they accept most anything. Through their involvement, they help the perpetrator build a façade. Personal impediment grows, ensnaring more individuals in dead-end traps. Entangled in the mess, willing participants are crippled in their ability to live free of constraints.

Where does this come from? To live with an unforgiving heart assures less productivity, along with an unclear, inaccurate focus. It diverts attention away from nurturing relationships and makes it difficult to live an authentically passionate life. Based on distorted truths, hardhearted critics readily believe what they think they see, shaped by a hoped-for glimpse to validate. In their world, seeing is believing rather than trusting what their eye cannot discern as those living by faith and in love.

The unforgiving may use their venom to harm another for any reason. Applied misdirection deflects viewing what is real in this small world. It is a useful tool that serves as justification for what is desired but never attained. The heart is shielded from seeing what the mind refuses to acknowledge. To selectively reject possibilities awaiting discovery as entirely impossible, hidden potential goes unrealized. The joy of unimaginable possibilities and fruitfulness are the real treasure for those living with compassion.

Truth, Lies, and Deception

Staged incidents create camouflage for lies and provide an adequate cover for those who feel the need for it. Have you ever noticed when people create issues where there are none? Some are so tender that the smallest offense is beyond their ability to bear. These opportunities give the perpetrator a feeling of strength and the desired appearance of control. They believe they are highly intelligent, superior in every way. They have convinced themselves they have earned the reputation for being able to defeat big problems in a single round.

When we step back from a problem, it becomes clear that much of a matter rests on unresolved personal issues for the instigator. We may see how those hanging on to their issues use them for as long as they like to stay in the public eye, to maintain credibility and stand ever vigilant. They appear to be in this battle, fighting it with full intention to win. At that moment, they cannot see their motivation is intrinsically intertwined with their being.

They attempt to battle it through ineffective means by exercising weak personal control. In essence, who they are is now clearly reflected by how they live their lives. Willing hearts with thinking minds can see this. It takes a fresh perspective and time. Forgiveness is the answer to the pain.

We probably know someone greatly wronged by a spouse. In the ashy aftermath, the injured held on to their offense. The hurt became their only remaining certainty in life. It was their new identity as they threw down who they used to be, now carrying this torment everywhere.

More than a cross to bear, this pain transforms into a new way of life. Maybe in a strange way it provides a hiding place, brought on by a fear of *what's next?* But hanging on to hurt serves as an obstacle in moving forward, living fully and productively.

No doubt it takes time to work through things, but the pain's permitted prominence in life and promises detrimental results. If the focus is always on what happened in the past, we can never live forward to what life will be.

Fear keeps us from being creative and all we can be. If it is allowed into our lives, our activities and enjoyment of all the things life offers, will be diminished. Opposing forces always encourage us to accept far less in every aspect of life. The Enemy attempts to do everything possible to keep us from getting closer to God.

Being aware of this, we must make a conscious effort to stand firm for what we believe. We live courageously in Jesus Christ by holding on to the truths we defend. This means maintaining the strength of our convictions, girded-up with a willingness to protect our position as necessary, even in the face of the most outrageous accusations or monstrous critics. Fortunately, we are never alone in this battle, as Scripture promises us (Hebrews 13:5).

Consider the case of longtime co-workers suddenly having difficulty in their working relationship. One of them feels offended by the other. An impaired working environment is the result. If productivity is negatively impacted, no matter the size of the issue hanging in the balance between the two, consequences could be dire. One (or both) could lose a job, be demoted, be reprimanded, or receive a penalty. Extending a pardon and attempting to work things out between working partners is worth avoiding a possible adverse outcome.

Sometimes when an offending coworker goes back to his associate to apologize, asking forgiveness with a heart to make a repair in that relationship (and it is accepted), the wounded continues to withhold grace in her mind and spirit.

Even when forgiveness is agreed upon, if the condition is ripe for an incident, the real or perceived wrong can live on in the heart or mind of the offended. It may somehow be leveraged for as long as possible, with the hope of receiving some greater reparation from the wrongdoer. Perhaps receiving continued sympathy from others or increased punishment for their perpetrator overrides their desire to move past this place.

The unforgiving spirit continues to grow in such cases, spreading like wildfire to colleagues and mutual friends, possibly for reasons beyond the original offense. It may be used to cover the victim's own tracks because he holds personal guilt for participating in the situation and knows their underlying motives.

It's much easier to toss it all onto someone else rather than acknowledge any personal responsibility for wrongdoing to family and friends. To hide the truth, scapegoating is easily accomplished. It is an ages-old technique to misdirect everyone's attention, especially when fueled by the desire to hide what could be considered a personally damaging incident or a highly compromising situation.

The longer this impasse goes on, the less it has to do with the offender or originating source of pain. Forgiveness takes time, but recognizing each party's role in an unfortunate turn of events is a significant sticking point. Maybe because it became an integral part of life and an extra layer fused onto our being, it is difficult to let go of, long after the matter is resolved. Meanwhile, unnecessary suffering continues, caused by the wrath unleashed by an unforgiving spirit.

Popular misconception fosters the idea that withholding love and grace secures *self* in a less vulnerable place. This seems to be a natural and practical thing we can easily do ourselves, while maintaining power over maligners in the face of things we cannot control.

This is in direct opposition to being believers relying on Jesus and living a life based on biblical principles.

Influenced by pop culture, this practice gives the immediate feeling of having an upper hand on a matter but is an ineffective, distorted, short-sighted action. In this way, we live twisted lives, wanting both unfettered freedoms to be all we can be yet holding on to what we perceive as a personal safeguard. Worse yet, we have given the unacceptable permission to coexist alongside us for as long as we allow.

This superior positioning prescribed by popular psychology turns out to be an unintentional stronghold. It effectively serves as an obstacle to all things positive we could ever hope for in life. Grace is the only solution to be free of these problems. If a matter is a continuing issue, we've already proven no other strategy works. If we find ourselves still struggling with a relational issue, our life will be negatively impacted by continuing problems in our relationships yet to be resolved. Heed the call.

It's hard to trust. People are broken. People are selfish, fickle, inconsistent, and not always truthful with one another. Have you ever experienced this?

We all have shortcomings that not one of us wants to admit, even to ourselves. But the truth is we must never place things, incidents, or others above Jesus, ranking them higher in order of importance, nor permitting their negative impact on us. We can, and must, follow His model if we are to live a peaceful, productive life. Forgiving is all about love. It is extending grace and living forward in freedom (Job 8:7).

Who are These Unforgiving Spirits?

Considering the havoc they create, it's easy to believe that perpetrators of nastiness are *bad* people or even monsters. Usually, they're regular human beings like you and me. Putting those who seemingly desire to inflict harm into a more comfortable personal frame of reference gives us permission to avoid them. This is an acknowledged context reserved for *evil* ones or those *crazies* to avoid.

In our perception, this knocks troublemakers down a few notches from the place of their desired greater importance. It puts them in a spot of lesser significance and influence in our lives. Laughing about it might lighten our mood but never solves the problem.

Reactions and motivations are tempered by human nature. Through false or incomplete information, we get the wrong idea about society or people. Because our insight or snippets gleaned are not accurate, we are served a small-slice view based on a quick peek, lightly seasoned with available talking points or sound bites. This skews our understanding and causes a rush to judgment. Misguided thinking makes us believe we can figure out a perplexing situation and determine the perfect solution for it. We've got this. Or so we think.

Our incredible minds are filled with unfathomable capabilities, the depths of which are yet to be discovered. Uniquely gifted by our gracious God, our great imagination, complex intelligence, and creative potential are only some of our recognized gifts. Although designed by God's great providence for good, these gifts can be (and are) used otherwise.

A side effect is a multitude of bewildering possibilities that occur using these gifts. Through their own imagination, fueled by deception and personal desires, misguided people create their own world entirely apart from others. Throughout time, we have repeatedly proven that where we focus our attention orients our lives. This becomes our true driving force, always impacting our capabilities and endeavors.

The variety of things we can think up is astonishing. From those thoughts, it is breathtaking how we can become thoroughly convinced that the most impossible situation is the absolute truth. Wholeheartedly believing whatever our minds can conceive or understand—taking what we believe is *true* and running with it—is simply lying to ourselves.

Fueled by feelings, our experiences, and sometimes with event-based timeline markers, we confidently give ourselves complete permission to accept our own distorted facts as truth, making them our reality.

A kind of legitimacy is granted to these meanderings of the mind when we internalize them. In doing so, we justify the state of our belief, shaping our lives and affecting the lives of others around us in powerful, sometimes unintentional ways.

A familiar example is when we convince ourselves our appearance is other than what it really is. We're sure we're fatter than we are. Maybe we know we're thinner, believing those jeans shrunk in the dryer. We think we're incredibly beautiful or undesirably unattractive.

Our analysis (which can be a form of idolatry) influences how we present ourselves and shapes our interactions with others. No matter how others treat us, the key factor within our innermost being is our belief that we have a purpose and we're somehow loved. These factors shape our personal world in expansive ways, whether they exist—or sadly, lack.

Accepting our distorted truth becomes our own misshapen reality. Maybe we're sure our genuine self is a camouflaged version of who we appear to be as we live a secret life inside, fearful of divulging this shocking fact to others. What we perceive, we believe to be true, readily accepting every far-reaching, powerful change that comes with this corrupted vision of who we are.

Perhaps forgiving ourselves is the hardest thing for us to do. Withholding forgiveness is a kind of personal punishment self-served due to feelings of inadequacy, something we regret doing, or something that should've-could've-would've been, if only things had been different.

Viewing things as they are in our reality is different through the lens of our heart. Removing layers of additional covering and stepping back from the heat of a moment, gives needed time and space to grasp the nuances of any situation.

By applying compassion, true empathy, and forbearance, it's possible to gain a more accurate awareness helpful in evaluating what has brought us to this place. This takes time, maybe even a lifetime.

Sometimes it's difficult to see things as they are when we fall into the abyss of stirring emotions and allow them to lead our lives:

• A sense of great loss may ignite flames of contention toward another. Distorted tales of "the one that got away" (traditionally a big whopper) are viewed by the lovelorn as an unhealed wound that forever festers on a hurting heart.

• Being overlooked for a perfect job opportunity, failure to win an election, never receiving recognition for noble efforts, or being publicly judged as falling short in the eyes of others, causes great emotional pain and fear of future consequences.

• Perhaps a lack of self-esteem is the fuse that lights a charge. In a small, personal world, putting another in their rightful place seems to be an impressive show of immense strength. Striking a match allows the one flexing relational muscles to maintain control over a situation, no matter how weak their position is. It remains their world. It *is* their world. Their rules allow them to win as *they* see it. This is not as it really is.

• Sometimes latent hate is targeted toward family members with the intent to damage familial ties. While nurtured roots of love may run deep, hostility among the ranks may be encouraged to maintain separation and to isolate. It may be created by an overblown slight perceived by a newcomer to the family. Lies or rumors are spread in a desire to refocus their spouse (maybe a sister, father, child) away from all others, entirely onto them.

•After remarrying, bitterness drives a stepparent because the children were not adopted nor fully accepted into the family. Maybe they are jealous or threatened by existing close family ties. Perhaps their attitude is caused by significant personal loss experienced, resulting in an inability to form meaningful relationships, still stinging from lingering hurts caused by past traumas.

- Unmet (or unrealistic) expectations and hidden fears may serve as a starting point for a barrage of hatred or hostility eventually unleashed upon another. The unfortunate person on the receiving end may be a spouse, friend, child, coworker, service professional, minister, social media network contact, or anyone the troubled person's path crosses. Accusations swirl. Misrepresentations and a campaign of unjustifiable, slanderous slurs are launched based on a tiny grain of truth but entirely blown out of proportion like the newest Urban Legend.
- Hatred and negativity are not the only influences harmful to relationships. When a parent loves a child too much, their relationship can become toxic. This occurs when everything centers on a child, due to fortunate (or unfortunate) circumstances. The parents seek to provide for the child's every need and comfort. We know this results in a spoiled child who will be ill-prepared for real life. This can turn deadly when a parent enables a child to continue their drug use or mistakenly trusts the child in ways beyond their ability, risking safety.

Isn't it surprising how often these kinds of incidents come to light? Even worse, it's shocking how long the relational thorn remains in place to cause unrelenting pain. Such situations have lasting impact on others well beyond the years the perpetrator is permitted to rule. The toxic environment sometimes extends well after their lifetime— unless the survivors are willing to take steps to make things right again.

Those readily embracing a crazy and confused paradigm as the way things are now, enable the unleashing of undeserved anguish on designated recipients. Acknowledged by those who appear somehow brainwashed, they blindly accept undesirable things as absolute fact.

All it takes is a semi-unconscious spouse, relative, or co-worker willing to accept their newly imposed reality.

As unwanted matters are thrust upon us, we always have a choice, even with no preparation or familiarity within the realm where we suddenly find ourselves. The steps we take, the words we use, and all actions that follow, are critically important. What seems unforgivable—and probably never asked for—brought us to this unpleasant place. We must recognize it for what it is before wending our way out of this mess. Our part in smoothing rough spots and receiving healing is in our control because it is determined by our actions.

It's easy to think an impossible situation has trapped us for life. But it's crucial for us to admit this thought is only one way to look at a troubling matter. Initially blindsided by the dread-filled unexpected leaves us feeling there is no way out. Surely there is no answer to a dilemma seemingly armed with the sole purpose of drowning us in total despair. It all becomes overwhelming only if we allow it.

Caught-up in the moment, we get carried away in black, swirling eddies. Spinning out of control, we struggle to stay afloat. The increasing drain on our strength to fight back rudely slaps at us and stings. Realizing our futility of escape becomes an undeniable shock. Panic sets in, adding an invisible weight to flailing legs. Keeping our head above dark waters now seems unimaginable. We know danger lurks ever near. We could so easily bob under these rushing currents, pulled downward one last time.

Real Life Assurances for an Uncertain World

Sometimes life situations unravel quickly. But our God is able. He is always present and consistent in His love and care. No problem, unresolved issue, or challenge is too much for Him to handle. Do you think your bewilderment is unique? The Bible covers every situation. The answer can be found there. Restoration is possible through prayerful conversation with our Father who wants to hear all about it.

God is not the author of confusion. If that's where you find yourself today, take a moment to consider where this chaos comes from. A thorn in our flesh as described by Paul (2 Corinthians 12:7-10), is a messenger of Satan. The discord directed at you is intended to throw you off course or out of the game entirely.

God made each of us for far more than we could ever imagine. We must hold to His higher standards. As Christians, we must never lower our standards to settle for less than God's best in life. We should remember that the world and Satan encourage us to embrace what is easy because it is a quick fix and less painful. This thorn is also an opportunity for us to see that (as Paul says in this passage), Jesus' grace is sufficient for all. In our times of weakness, we are made secure through Him, for Christ's sake.

Given the slightest opportunity, hellfire-heated false conclusions can blow-up even the smallest matters to enormous proportions, well beyond the reasonable bounds of logic. Isn't it just like humans to be highly confident in self-designated capabilities of being all-knowing? The truth is we don't have our own solutions or even a grain of supreme intelligence. If you doubt this, look around and notice the disastrous results of applying our own understanding to fix the brokenness in our lives.

It's easy to become overwhelmed in turbulent times. We feel as if we're tossed about on relentless waves when we lose a clear perspective of who God is to us. Recognizing He is the master craftsman who can make complete restorations, we know He can restore our most painful, broken relationships, and knit lost family members right back into the picture. He can make things right. He can use evil for good in the most unexpected ways.

Jesus reminds us that our faith in Him, even the size of a tiny mustard seed, makes all the difference (Matthew 17: 20).

God doesn't rework things for a new, improved version. He doesn't reform the aberrant, making modifications to fix only the broken parts. In a stroke of pure genius the world can never replicate, He masterfully accomplishes complete restorations based on His original, unchanging plan. This is no renovation, redecoration, or revise of an old familiar favorite. Left in His hands to do His artful work, He returns it (and us) to its (our) original, intended lustrous state (2 Corinthians 13:11).

Are you sitting here with me, reading this book, thinking you'll get this mess figured out somehow, sometime soon? Maybe you intended to get this done before now, but it just hasn't happened. I know it seems unimaginable, but it's worthwhile to consider that it's possible one day you (or someone you know) might be struck with a dreaded disease or a debilitating condition stops you in your tracks of making things right again.

With all your heart, you always planned to get around to doing this hard thing called forgiving, but now ... you're incapable. Maybe the person cannot be reached due to ill health, or perhaps they died. The words won't come, and maybe the tears will, but no one will ever know why, and you can't say. Your intent of the heart is locked inside, and you're leaving a messy legacy that will live on forever. You know essential things are left undone. A sea of regret lies before you, lapping up around your ankles as you walk alone along the dark, rocky shoreline.

Even if you somehow know this scenario is impossible, why wait? There has never been a time like now. Today's a great day to forgive. It's possible today and can begin right now. Using God's uncommon sense to guide your life will help you through this process. His way is time-tested and true. Countless testimonies of others have proven that following Him works and promises long-lasting effects.

Through God's grace for our sins, we are forgiven and free. We are God's beloved children, no longer held as a slave to the past. We are heirs of His kingdom. We have a mandate for action. Realizing time is precious and limited, every moment we cling to our crumbling fortress of unforgiveness or allow ourselves to remain behind those walls steals from our time to enjoy life on this earth. We are withholding blessings God has planned for us by not living His way (Jeremiah 28:11). We must allow ourselves to grow beyond it, seeing a broader, big-picture view. It's important to remember no matter how long we live, our time on earth is short.

Our need for safety is fueled by the desire for order and control. Personal security is an inherent desire in human existence. It shapes our actions. We may feel secure by remaining in the comfortable position posed by a problem because we know it well. To take action might cause extreme discomfort and put us in a place we're not equipped to handle. This unknown creates fear, uncertainty, and insecurity.

Recognizing dustups cause life messes to deal with, we risk upending our current life. In light of this, we willingly live in this imperfect way. We trade freedom for accepting known problems and offending situations, accommodated by our pieced-together life.

But the concept of security is merely an illusion, a figment of our imagination. We fool ourselves when we live a lie we fabricated as a form of insulation around us. It doesn't exist. God is the rock of all creation, and He provides real security to those who seek Him (Deuteronomy 31:6). Touch points throughout history include recorded events that show He does exist. Faith is required to rest in this place. Isn't it curious how that which we cannot see [God] is the one, right, real relationship we need?

The Bible promises He will always be with us (Deuteronomy 31:8). We can cling to Him as inevitable storm waters splash and rush around us. His presence remains with us always as a place of refuge. He steadfastly stands with us, an unchanging foundation of unmatched strength, still offering reliable support and guidance when we ask.

His unparalleled wisdom provides elegant and innovative solutions to life's stickiest situations. If you don't believe me, just listen to some of the testimonies shared by those who've navigated these uncertain waters, and you'll see for yourself. Many of the incredible stories you will hear describe people who have beaten all odds, even with the deck stacked against them in a game dealt by a blackleg.

These are tall tales of menacing and intimidating forces. looming at every turn. Not even a glimmer of hope is discernible to the human eye. But apparently, it is seen off in the distance by the human heart, filled with the sincere desire to see. It's there. It's always there. And so is God. He's waiting (Mark 11:24).

Forgiving in Real Life: Apply the Principles and Live these Truths by Reflection Challenge

Ultimately, living the kind of life God wants for us is not up to our cleverness or personal ability. It is through living in faith and relying on God to always intercede on our behalf at every twist and turn we encounter.

Unforgiving spirits cause physical, emotional, and spiritual problems that create bitterness, anger, and hate. Living life as our Father wants us to is where our spiritual rubber meets the road.

Action steps

Will you go the distance?

How will you choose to willingly participate with Him today?

NINE
LOVING BEYOND THE HARD PLACES

Loving Beyond Difficulties Will Bring You Through Them

If we study God's Word as related to how we should treat others, it's easy to see how following His example is the most effective way to nurture and enjoy fellowship. This creates deep, richly meaningful relationships with those closest to us.

This we know:
- God is all about relationship. He created us to know, love, and fellowship with Him. From the beginning, this was His plan. (Genesis 1:1, 2: 26-28)
- Sin impairs our relationship with God and our ability to forgive others by creating a break that needs restoration. (Genesis 3:9)
- God created mankind with free will to accept and love Him—or not. (Romans 10:9-10)
- God always loves us, every day of our lives. (1 Corinthians 1:9)
- Loving God means we put Him first in our lives. (1 Thessalonians 2:12)

. . .

Adam and Eve's Fall Shows Us God's Enduring Grace and Love

The story of Adam and Eve in the Garden of Eden documents man's first sin (Genesis 3:4-7). A close look at this event tells us a lot about God, His grace, and how forgiveness works. He provided for this couple's every need, gave them purpose, and laid out some simple ground rules (Genesis 2:8-9, 15-19). Eve saw the enticing fruit on the Tree of Knowledge of Good and Evil. Even facing the possibility of death, she was influenced as the cunning serpent encouraged her to ignore what God said about not eating from it. It all seemed to make perfect sense. How could eating this fruit hurt anything? So, she ate some. Helpmate that she was, Eve shared it with Adam. This simple act of disobedience caused their fall from God's favor, with a ripple-effect for all mankind.

Isn't it fascinating how the thing we want most, our greatest desire of this moment, is precisely the thing we shouldn't have? The distraction we pursue at all costs is usually something we know we're not to enjoy. Intrigue with seeking the forbidden can be fueled by addiction, obsession, curiosity, pride, or desire for control. Whenever emotions rule, they justify making bad decisions and doing wrong things.

Swayed by the serpent's cunningness, Adam and Eve willfully disregarded God's instruction because they reasoned it would be beneficial to them. Let's make no mistake. This was a high-stakes decision, risking life to gain something they felt entitled to have. God sought them out from their shameful hiding place and asked for their side of the story. He listened but never interjected His thoughts about the matter to them directly as they told their tale (Genesis 3:8-13).

Once it was clearly established they had sinned—regardless of the influences or circumstances surrounding their wrongdoing—the couple was held accountable by God. In their disobedience, Adam and Eve sinned, and they suffered the consequences of their actions. It's interesting to note the resulting punishment was not death but a banishment from their beautifully blessed life to one that was much more difficult (Genesis 3:22-24). This shows grace extended to Adam and Eve—they lived. It also shows punishment and grace are swift and sure by our loving God (Genesis 3:14-20). But His grace didn't stop there. He provided further for them by making garments of skin to clothe them before sending them out into the world (Genesis 3:21).

Four stunning thoughts popped into my mind as I studied this story:
- We never see a mention of Adam or Eve's personal admission of guilt, an apology, nor gratefulness for God's grace.
- The ever-popular blame game began with the first sin as Eve credits the serpent for her sinful decision. Then Adam blames Eve.
- Lying to cover up true motivations, paired with the blame game, is a losing strategy. Clearly, God already knew their rationale.
- Conclusion: Apparently, knowing about good and evil still hasn't helped mankind live better lives.

According to Scripture, God's removal of the erring couple from their comfortable post in that beautiful garden not only reset their lives but also ours. God's relocation plan for Adam and Eve nipped all that in the bud, banishing them off to a whole new world and way of life. This brilliant move paved the only one true way to having everlasting life to be through Jesus Christ.

While the world has inherent evil and temptations that misrepresent themselves as golden opportunities, relying on God's directives and His gift of discernment allows safer passage. Sometimes our mistake is putting ourselves in a wrong place or listening to others instead of seeking His guidance.

Like Adam, the extent of our involvement may be as an innocent bystander when something bad happens. Unfortunately, there will be resulting consequences, but His grace is always available. Our Lord and Savior Jesus Christ is always present, waiting to bring us through. He will catch us at our next slip or fall. He is our Redeemer.

Adam and Eve's story shows us exactly what God's grace and forgiveness are about:

- He is clear about wanting to maintain His relationship with us and will do whatever it takes to keep us close.
- He already knows what's weighing on our hearts, what we've done, and why, but wants to hear from us.
- He wants to keep our conversation going with Him through our constant fellowship and prayer.
- He wants us to see and admit where we've made mistakes and know they can be forgiven.
- Once admitted, our wrongs will not be belabored in ongoing admonition from Him, but life consequences and changes result.
- His forgiveness always gives us a fresh start ... a new life. It will be different, but He remains the same and is there to meet us. We can begin again.
- God's love is constant for every one of us. His immense love extends well beyond the hard places in our life.

Forgiving in Real Life

Once the forgiveness process begins, if we bravely leave ourselves open to personal discovery, we see a layer of complications we can remove from life. We discover the need for forgiving ourselves for hanging on to our unforgiving attitude, which stands in the way of restoration. Possibly, we fooled ourselves into believing our lives were insulated by withholding grace, creating a comfortable distance from the pain of a situation.

Mistakenly, we believed we were in charge of dispensing forgiveness on troubling matters, enjoying the regal throne of personal power we built for ourselves. In the end, we discover when we go our own way instead of God's we lock ourselves up in our own spiritual prison. Our constant companion called *unforgiveness* is forever chained next to us.

Maybe the problem is daunting. It seems too big to deal with, leaving us afraid and shaken to our innermost core. But the truth is we are not alone in this. We already know God promised He would never leave us. In His incredible love for us He provides all we need, although we may not at first see how (Colossians 3: 12-15):

So, chosen by God for this new life of love, dress in the wardrobe God picked out for you: compassion, kindness, humility, quiet strength, discipline. Be even-tempered, content with second place, quick to forgive an offense. Forgive as quickly and completely as the Master forgave you. And regardless of what else you put on, wear love. It's your basic, all-purpose garment. Never be without it. Let the peace of Christ keep you in tune with each other, in step with each other. None of this going off and doing your own thing. And cultivate thankfulness.

Living in Truth, Loving Beyond this Pain

What do forgiving Christians look like? Sometimes it's realizing the person (maybe a parent) did the best they could, after all. They are not perfect any more than we are. People who intentionally treat others badly do so for lack of something they perceive in their lives. This may be due to something they've done or experienced. At times, people feel threatened, lack confidence, or don't want to see things change—and you challenge all of that in their world. This happens in families, at school, in groups of friends, and at church, to name a few instances.

Forgiving is not accepting bad behavior or justifying it by saying we understand (even when we don't). We may never make sense of the mess. Knowing whatever haunted them that made life as it was when it collided with ours—while possibly influencing their treatment—may never hold the entire answer. It's not up to us to know, but God does. Forgiving them is up to us by recognizing what happened, while the one causing the incident is held accountable. Forgiving means extending grace to the wrongdoer while knowing we would have liked things to be different.

Reflecting on all this, and studying the forgiveness story of Adam and Eve, I know I have gotten through my most challenging times by loving beyond the hard places.

Loving beyond the pain is:
- Hoping for the best and extending grace even when it's not.
- Knowing nothing will be perfect during our earthly lives but will *be* just as it is.
- Realizing a situation may never be restored to the extent it could be but not letting the grief of recognized lost potential be burdensome.
- Loving courageously even in the face of indifference, hate, or rejection—and never giving up.
- Never embracing another's thoughts, relational limitations, or unacceptable treatment as personal truth, worth, or purpose.

All of us have lived with the consequences of decisions and actions personally made, as well as those by others in our life. Hope is alive, and transformation is always possible. Nearly half a lifetime later, I have been blessed with my own loving family and our beautiful life together. I am sincerely grateful for all of it and counting it all joy.

Hebrews 8:12-13 illustrates our Father's grace lovingly extended to all His children. It represents a new covenant made with us by God. When Jesus Christ died on the cross for forgiveness of our sins, we received salvation. We are forgiven and free. We need not do anything more than accept His priceless gift. It's reassuring to know God has pardoned us to the extent that He promises to never again remember our sin. He's not keeping a list of all our slip-ups and mistakes. He isn't constantly nagging, always reminding us, "do you remember the time when you ..."

If day-to-day activities or sleepless nights are interrupted with dark fleeting thoughts and pain-filled reminders of wrongs, this is not from God. If a reminder of something left undone comes to mind, it may be Him pointing out something that needs to be addressed. He assured us He will not remember our past wrongdoings because we are forgiven. Pray about what's troubling you. Seek His guidance on the matter. Do what you can to find resolution, receive forgiveness, extend grace to another, and put the matter to rest.

God's Word signifies a new covenant He established with His people. There are changes in how things will be done. A truly remarkable sign of God's love and forgiveness is how His son Jesus Christ died in such a public way for our salvation. It is truly the ultimate sacrifice. Remarkably, Jesus' death and resurrection are still remembered today by nonbelievers as well as believers.

Old Testament practices and traditions no longer apply. For example, animal sacrifices are not required (nor accepted) as a sign of faith. As Christ followers, we are invited to enjoy the abundance of food available on the earth with no restrictions placed on us (Hebrews 9:22-28).

We don't need to sacrifice our lives or relationships with those we love by not forgiving past sins or wrongs done. This new covenant with God also releases all heirs from carrying the burdens of their predecessors with them into their present lives, as was customary in Old Testament times. Applying this today, families of perpetrators of wrongful acts are not responsible for their ancestors' misdeeds. There is accountability for the one who does the deed, and they are the ones who carry the responsibility.

It's easy to see how families of the wrongdoers may carry a burden of shame, feeling guilty by association. It's human nature to feel this way, but as believers we have to accept the fact that God will deal with malefactors and can use even bad things for His good in our lives.

It may be difficult to remove ourselves from the wrongs someone we know well or who is close to us has done. It is not God's design for us to carry their wrongs forward into our lives, unnecessarily suffering in any way for the actions of another.

The familiar expression "Let go and let God" is a bit of a misnomer. Similar to the adage "forgive and forget," it is in part true because we recognize that God has the upper hand over all creation, no matter what anyone thinks. In our relationship with Him, we have to allow Him to handle all matters, leading and guiding us according to His will. As His followers, we must be willing participants in His plan, following His precepts and prompts. We already know He has our best in mind.

Romans 10:4-10 assures us of this:

The earlier revelation was intended simply to get us ready for the Messiah, who then puts everything right for those who trust him to do it. Moses wrote that anyone who insists on using the law code to live right before God soon discovers it's not so easy—every detail of life regulated by fine print. But trusting God to shape the right living in us is a different story—no precarious climb up to heaven to recruit the Messiah, no dangerous descent into hell to rescue the Messiah. So, what exactly was Moses saying?

The word that saves is right here,
> as near as the tongue in your mouth,
> as close as the heart in your chest.

It's the word of faith that welcomes God to go to work and set things right for us. This is the core of our preaching. Say the welcoming word to God—"Jesus is my Master"—embracing, body and soul, God's work of doing in us what he did in raising Jesus from the dead. That's it. You're not "doing" anything; you're simply calling out to God, trusting him to do it for you. That's salvation. With your whole being you embrace God setting things right, and then you say it, right out loud: "God has set everything right between him and me."

Grace 24/7: Through the Power of One

Extending grace means to be humble, with a servant's heart. This is exhibited by how we live and put others before ourselves. But before that, it requires us to put God first and let Him guide and direct each step. It is only through the power of our one God that grace is available 24/7. We can't do this alone. Haven't we already proven to ourselves that doing forgiveness our own way doesn't work? It's much harder to endure the pain for longer than necessary when we insist on ignoring forgiveness and grace done His way, rather than ours.

In Philippians 2:1-16, Paul tells us how to treat others, remain obedient to our Father, and what all this looks like:

He Took on the Status of a Slave

If you've gotten anything at all out of following Christ, if his love has made any difference in your life, if being in a community of the Spirit means anything to you, if you have a heart, if you *care*—then do me a favor: Agree with each other, love each other, be deep-spirited friends. Don't push your way to the front; don't sweet-talk your way to the top. Put yourself aside, and help others get ahead. Don't be obsessed with getting your own advantage. Forget yourselves long enough to lend a helping hand.

Think of yourselves the way Christ Jesus thought of himself. He had equal status with God but didn't think so much of himself that he had to cling to the advantages of that status no matter what. Not at all. When the time came, he set aside the privileges of deity and took on the status of a slave, became *human*. Having become human, he stayed human. It was an incredibly humbling process. He didn't claim special privileges. Instead, he lived a selfless, obedient life and then died a selfless, obedient death—and the worst kind of death at that—a crucifixion.

Because of that obedience, God lifted him high and honored him far beyond anyone or anything, ever, so that all created beings in heaven and on earth—even those long ago dead and buried—will bow in worship before this Jesus Christ, and call out in praise that he is the Master of all, to the glorious honor of God the Father. (v 1-11)

Make no mistake, forgiveness is never a gift we can give ourselves. Forgiveness is the gift God gives us if we are willing to accept it. Because He first loved us, we can love others.

Rejoicing Together

What I'm getting at, friends, is that you should simply keep on doing what you've done from the beginning. When I was living among you, you lived in responsive obedience. Now that I'm separated from you, keep it up. Better yet, redouble your efforts. Be energetic in your life of salvation, reverent and sensitive before God. That energy is *God's* energy, an energy deep within you, God himself willing and working at what will give him the most pleasure.

Do everything readily and cheerfully—no bickering, no second-guessing allowed! Go out into the world uncorrupted, a breath of fresh air in this squalid and polluted society. Provide people with a glimpse of good living and of the living God. Carry the light-giving Message into the night so I'll have good cause to be proud of you on the day that Christ returns. You'll be living proof that I didn't go to all this work for nothing. (v 12-16)

. . .

Forgiving in Real Life: Apply the Principles and Live these Truths by Personal Reflection

Trust comes through truth. True brotherly love is a willingness to be honest and kind. When we free our relationships from anger, there's more room for love and life (Ephesians 4:26). Isn't it wonderful to imagine our celebration as we rejoice in restoring a broken relationship? What a party it will be! It may take a lifetime to have that party, but every step closer to it is worth celebrating.

Action Step

Imagine how will you celebrate.

TEN
LIFE IS A GRACE-FILLED ADVENTURE

Our Future is Not Found in the Past

We receive instruction and our heavenly Father's assurance for our journey of restoration in Isaiah 43:18-19:

Forget about what's happened; don't keep going over old history. Be alert, be present. I'm about to do something brand-new. It's bursting out. Don't you see it? There it is. I'm making a road through the desert, rivers in the badlands.

Maybe you've arrived at a place in life where things have to change because the way things are now is not working for anyone. Deep in your heart you know the situation is not right. It's clear a change has to be made. As you consider the troubled relationship, it becomes intolerable. Life is filled with disappointments.

. . .

Many of our deepest wounds are caused by relationship woes. Here are a few:

• Parents are crushed to discover their child is living a secret life so abhorrent it's impossible to trace what drew them into that dark place. They never saw it coming.

• A void grows after many years of marriage when a spouse's infidelity during their child-rearing days is found out.

• Feelings of inadequacy persist because no one cared enough.

• Always called unworthy, there was never a chance.

• Others could never see far enough beyond their own problems to encourage great things in others.

• Disregarding a spouse's determination and following the Lord's leading in work for His kingdom, a doubting spouse expresses lack of respect, believing it is worthless.

Thinking of examples of good relationships, we know healthy ones naturally exhibit mutual respect, shared love, care, and concern for one another. Relationships require more than one person. They are dynamic in nature. Even when joined as one heart, a true relationship includes more than one mind, multiple talents, gifts, and different passions into the mix. This is when things become interesting.

Nurturing a relationship requires understanding. Even being of the same accord, pursuit, or shared end-goal—within established confines or connections (marriage or work)— differences are generally accepted as complimentary and never used for harm. These differences can be harnessed for positive results. My husband and I learned in the early years of our marriage that two thinking minds working together are better than just one in decision-making.

Partners in a relationship may look at something differently and go about the process of consideration in vastly unique ways yet still merge perspectives to successfully develop the best conclusion or answer.

Recognizing the inherent foibles of human nature, we know when conflict occurs in relationships, asking for or extending forgiveness is required. It is hurtful when something is purposefully swept out of sight by a trusted someone in our life, with apparent hope of it never being discovered.

Deception encourages a slow death to relationships. When deceit is discovered, it poisons trust, which is foundational to build and sustain any type of relationship. Still, it happens and must be dealt with, or we remain stuck in this uncomfortable place.

Calling for change is daunting. Perhaps those you need to speak with are dominating personalities or have major control issues that rule life. Maybe you feel like young David taking on mighty Goliath, against all odds (1 Samuel 17:1-51). But unlike David, dread fills you with fear as you figure you have no chance of seeing this matter through to resolution without suffering severe personal damage and more intense pain. You know something must change because the situation makes living a full life impossible.

The Enemy will lay traps to foil attempts for freedom. Thinking of the ordeal that lies ahead, terrible things imagined can intimidate us, creating a facade of formidable circumstances.

Fearing more pain is usually enough to make anyone flee the scene. Our human nature is played on by Satan himself as he reminds us how *worthy* we are, assuring us we can easily control this situation, simply walk away from it, or ignore those involved. We are convinced we can set up a brand-new life and no one will ever know. The problem is this is all untrue because it did happen, and the fallout caused still exists.

There is simply no way around it and no way to get over it. The only way through is with our Lord of lords Jesus Christ at our side.

In Luke 9:23b, Jesus promises to lead us and show us how to stand with Him:

Anyone who intends to come with me has to let me lead.

You're not in the driver's seat—I am. Don't run from suffering; embrace it. Follow me and I'll show you how. Self-help is no help at all. Self-sacrifice is the way, my way, to finding yourself, your true self. What good would it do to get everything you want and lose you, the real you? If any of you is embarrassed with me and the way I'm leading you, know that the Son of Man will be far more embarrassed with you when he arrives in all his splendor in company with the Father and the holy angels. This isn't pie in the sky by and by. Some who have taken their stand right here are going to see it happen, see with their own eyes the kingdom of God.

Strength for the Journey

In the early days of my career as I was establishing my consultancy, I began running. My running led to participating in area road races. Eventually, I developed a full-fledged personal cross-training program. I did win a few races in my age group but running remained my least favorite part of working out. While running, I sometimes wondered why I did. I kept running anyway.

Through the encouragement of friends, I learned I was gifted to run for long periods of time. This made sense, because I easily biked and swam long distances, faster than most runners. In college dance classes, I learned I had the right muscles for sustained movement. God made me able to continue in motion for long periods of time, competing with endurance. Sometimes I felt as if working out was like taking inner strength and applying it to my outer self.

When we are on the journey toward relational restoration, seeking forgiveness or grace from another, we need to remember the path is uncertain. Hazards exist, and there is no promised outcome for running the race. We might even wonder why we're running and how long this run will take us—but we keep running anyway.

Unlike running a road race, finish time is not a factor in this jaunt to forgiveness. We all need to run a long, slow distance in order to finish. Time and care need to be taken intentionally as we consider others involved.

Seeking forgiveness and extending grace should not be considered a race. Each situation takes as much time as it requires to be completed. This is a difficult thing for most of us today, even for the most patient. We are accustomed to stories resolving themselves by the end of a movie. Answers to life's most pressing questions can be found in a quick online search, while a week's worth of groceries can be purchased with a click and a credit card. How long could this forgiveness thing take? For some, it takes a lifetime.

Our heart's desire to make things right can be a powerful influence to propel us forward in mending broken relationships. We may indeed slay insurmountable odds if we are willing to go the distance. If we are brave enough to move forward in our quest to set things right, it's possible to see some change. Sometimes we must patiently await the signal to begin a run—as we anxiously toe the starting line—hoping our training has prepared us for this race.

One afternoon during the week (half a lifetime ago), I received a phone call from my mother. When she was diagnosed with pancreatic cancer, our family's life as we knew it changed dramatically for all of us. We always stood ready for a phone call, or the next trip (soon) to visit her. Somehow, this call seemed different from the outset. We had a pleasant conversation, both of us updating the other with our latest. In addition to my business running along well at full speed, I was planning a simple wedding three months from then. I'm sure all my activities were highly predictable and no doubt mundane, especially compared to the cancer rollercoaster she had been on.

We talked for as long as she felt energy enough to speak. Just before we said our *goodbyes* and *I love you*, she paused to apologize for "always putting me last." I was so taken by surprise I couldn't catch my breath and didn't know what to say. Realizing the gravity of the moment, I scrambled for the most gracious words I knew, to reassure her the best way I could that all was well and I loved her. This was our last conversation.

I've replayed that phone call and her finishing words over and over in my heart many times. I've held them close. I've marveled at them. I treasure them. I remember the feeling of the call. It was calm and filled with peace. The sound of her voice seemed to reflect her spirit as somehow different than at any time before. The words were not words she would have normally said to anyone, and yet she spoke them to me. She gave voice to what I never dared to think. Clearly, there was a heart transformation. Forgiveness took place that day, and grace was extended in authentic love.

Friend, are you in a difficult situation, thinking you cannot possibly forgive? I urge you to contemplate Matthew 12:31-32:

There's nothing done or said that can't be forgiven. But if you deliberately persist in your slanders against God's Spirit, you are repudiating the very One who forgives. If you reject the Son of Man out of some misunderstanding, the Holy Spirit can forgive you, but when you reject the Holy Spirit, you're sawing off the branch on which you're sitting, severing by your own perversity all connection with the One who forgives.

I found this passage of Scripture to be both shocking and compelling. Admittedly, we do know slandering God's name (blasphemy) is an unforgivable offense, so that did not surprise me (entire portion of this passage included for clarity). But the rest of it is shocking to me because it does seem like some things are unforgivable, doesn't it?

According to Jesus, this is not the case at all if we are truly one of His followers. Does this make you stop in your tracks and think, *But wait a minute. That awful thing happened to me. I should have full control over how I handle this.* While we may have our free will to choose our actions and behaviors, Jesus makes it clear His followers do not have the freedom to withhold forgiveness for any reason, nor to dispense it only when and if we choose to do so. By viewing His words from this perspective, I am convicted to make my way toward forgiveness by extending grace in all circumstances. He is in charge, and we do not wield the power of forgiveness over anyone—including ourselves. To think or do otherwise is to fully embrace the world's losing ways.

Jesus does not give us a timeline or mandated period for when resolution must be reached. Did you notice this too? In considering His instruction, I don't think this gives us license to carry our unforgiving attitudes forward, because every minute of that is intentionally living in direct opposition of keeping God's directives. His ways may be far more challenging for us to accomplish, and usually run counterintuitive to our crazy human logic, but they are always appropriate, and the blessings will come when we follow Him.

What Could Be is Exciting

Do you long for things to be improved in your relationships? Do you wish your life were completely different from what it is right now? Through grace, we know people can change. That change does not come by our actions, but rather through Christ who strengthens us to do the right things to help us on the way to restoration.

Our lives transform when we become relentlessly determined to live God's way instead of our own. Transformation comes when we change our heart, see things differently, live intentionally, and love radically. By choosing to live fully committed by pressing on through hardships and rejecting worldly ways as Christ followers, it becomes entirely possible to see our way more clearly toward peace and grace.

Yet for all our dedicated efforts, our hope for better days may never be fully achieved. Our heartfelt desire to mend a broken relationship may take a lifetime. Possibly, we will never see complete resolution with one harboring inherent control issues. Not permitting us to get closer than mere platitudes and impersonal generalities, we remain held at arm's length.

Fear of life changes that result if the line drawn in the sand were erased, the possibility of growing closer immobilizing. They prefer to maintain life as it is. Being surrounded by pain and loss provides a strange form of familiar comfort because it allows personal control over disturbing life issues. Unfortunately, they don't realize what they're missing. But you do.

Whether a broken relationship involves faltering Christians or non-Christians, modeling Christlike behavior shows others how grace is extended and relationships can be mended. It also helps us in the process (as Jesus promises). We must treat others as the unique individuals they are, not as a member of some labeled people-group touted by the world. Relationships are personal and one-on-one. Strong bonds are developed with each person. Built through trust and forged with love, restoration takes time.

It's important to remember forgiveness is not so much about what we do to make things happen ourselves. It isn't all about us. All our wishing, waiting, hoping, praying, and doing may or may never play any part in true restoration. Staying the course and persevering in authentic attempts to rebuild a relationship does.

My story about the last conversation with my adopted mother is a great illustration of Jesus' presence in that relationship. I believe He was there the entire time. He knew all about our situation—from before I was born to when her last breath on earth would be. He knew the desires of our hearts and our great need for restoration, forgiveness, grace, and peace. That day, He delivered it to us. It was a sacred moment. This is possible for you in your situation as well.

Word of Caution

If we were to meet over coffee, sharing heart-to-heart about life today, I imagine we'd agree we're living in interesting times. One thing frequently arising in conversations today is DNA testing used to determine family heritage. I won't get into my personal thoughts about the process, but I will agree it's an intriguing concept.

The desire to discover family roots by DNA testing or establish legacy through old-school family tree research is an enduring pursuit for many. Finding answers, discovering long-held secrets, and making sought-after connections becomes a sort of personal holy grail for those who deep-dive into data banks and dusty tomes. Dedicated exploration is always rewarded with each nugget uncovered, or every interesting bit of information revealed is a potential source of family pride (or disgrace).

Delving into our origins is not for the faint of heart. Digging deep into the past can uncover the unexpected. Maybe we discover a relative in the 1800s was a horse thief who was hung for his crime in England. Or perhaps we unearth a new and exciting extension of the family.

Through our research, study, and testing, we may dispel long-held family myths, casting aside our shared fanciful legend and lore for provable truths that serve as mile markers along the road to knowing who we really are.

As an adopted kid, discovering my DNA would probably have answered a few questions for me, but I never asked. From the time I was a young child, I accepted my private adoption before birth as part of God's plan for my life. While it has driven some friends around me mad with wondering, I accepted this as fact long ago.

Personally, I've always enjoyed living free of labels. I am free to be. I cannot fathom what it would be like to know who my relatives are beyond my family today. Although family resemblances of those I know have always fascinated me, I've never longed for that.

The life given us here on earth is a blessing from our Father. He has provided for us, gifting each with a purpose for being and our own unique plan. We have also been given free will to accept Him and His priceless gift of salvation or go our own way. We can live our lives wishing, waiting, and hoping things will turn out as we want. Our entire focus can be toward finally getting that one thing we know will make our life complete. We rationalize that reaching a certain point will make us truly happy.

A pop culture question that continues to surface gives me pause:

Who's your daddy? Sadly, there are some children in this world who were not adopted like me who cannot answer this for other reasons. (In my case, I have no idea who my birth mother is, either.) I would suppose that is why this question became so popular, used as an insensitive joke among the mainstream (who likely do know their parents). I believe it is a haunting reality for those who contemplate it, never knowing the answer but deep-down wishing they did.

Our quest for personal happiness, gain, knowledge, and status never ends. Rarely do our tireless efforts give us the results we think they should. At some point we may see that part of the reason we continue our futile attempt is fueled by something we've done or experienced. Perhaps we recognize we've allowed it to hold us back or incite an undesirable reaction as reflected by our lives. With a dose of clarity, we can see a change to make things right is needed.

The yearning to make a necessary relational repair is influenced by a transformed heart. Restoration may begin by admitting a mistake needs to be corrected. A growing desire to see this through produces the will to administer tender loving care to a relational break crying for attention.

Finding ourselves at a crossroad fighting through personal guilt and shame to forgive ourselves, we recognize moving forward means we can let go of the unnecessary baggage holding us back.

We can buy a DNA family history package to learn about our personal heritage, but we will never know who our true Father is if we don't seek Him. We can contact long-lost relatives and experience the great joy of deeper connections with our kin all over the globe, but we will never truly restore life's broken places if we don't follow Him. The truth is we all have a Father in heaven who loves each of us very much. How wonderful we are all adopted into His family.

He made room for all of us. He desires a close relationship and wants us to keep Him in our lives. He wants us to love others and endeavor to get along well with everyone. He loves us beyond what we could ever know. Unlike those times when we are ready to throw in the towel on a relationship, He will never give up on us or on His desire to hold us close. His pursuit of us continues throughout our lives, right up to our last breath. We can all know who our Father is.

So that little girl (me) given up for adoption and three times rejected by her own adoptive family, was indelibly blessed with a far better perspective of it all as she realized it was God's plan for her. Know this, I praise God for His redeeming grace and immense love. I always knew it, and I never stopped praying, but did occasionally ask Him "what were you thinking here?" In part, I believe it was to bless me with a wonderful family I never knew I wanted (as a too-busy, successful entrepreneur consultant) until I was married and we had our two sons.

The other part of this blessing is so I could meet you here to tell you of God's love and forgiveness. I share this with you to show His love and grace is everything—and that you, like me, can do this. You can forgive, extending grace to others and to yourself. God has something more in store for you. Never settle for less.

How well we know that God's ways are not ours. Yet as followers of Jesus, we must embrace His higher standards. In doing so, we will never sell ourselves short, forfeit our blessing, or settle for less than our Father's best for our lives.

We are so blessed. Luke 6:20b-23 confirms this:

You're blessed when you've lost it all. God's kingdom is there for the finding. You're blessed when you're ravenously hungry. Then you're ready for the Messianic meal. You're blessed when the tears flow freely. Joy comes with the morning.

Count yourself blessed every time someone cuts you down or throws you out, every time someone smears or blackens your name to discredit me. What it means is that the truth is too close for comfort and that that person is uncomfortable. You can be glad when that happens—skip like a lamb, if you like—for even though they don't like it, I do ... and all heaven applauds. And know that you are in good company; my preachers and witnesses have always been treated like this.

Through His grace and peace, by following His ways, we can see how wonderful things could be. I believe He lights our way and gives us hope as we love our way forward. For all the stories of forgiveness, and those unfortunate circumstances that never reach restoration, there is always one thing we can (and must) do without fail: *forgive*.

In the case of risking safety, personal contact may be unadvisable, but prayer is always appropriate. As discussed before, we can forgive someone even if we never personally see them again due to their death, incarceration, or not having them present in our lives for any reason. They don't have to know about it nor accept our grace, but we can and must wholeheartedly extend it to them ourselves through prayer and living our lives forward in love.

At no point are we given the option to give up or think we've done all we can while the problem continues to fester. We cannot acquiesce to behaviors or situations that are not God honoring, are hurtful, or create a divide in relationships. Turning our backs or letting go of a painful situation is the same as giving permission for it to continue.

As we passively complain in our quietest voice on the sidelines of a skirmish, we allow it to continue to exist. By not continuing our attempt to resolve the matter, we can never truthfully say it wasn't our choice, decision, or doing. We furthered it by enabling the conflict creator and giving him free reign. In our heart, we know this is true. In a relationship we simply must show up regularly, sharing care and compassion. By remaining present and personally available, we remain open to the possibility of better things.

Of course, I'm not advocating stalking someone, knocking their door down every other day, or calling them day and night. Our best course of action is always using Jesus as our model for building relationships and restoring our brokenness. Where would we be if He didn't relentlessly pursue us? We should be living in grace and truth as a continued compassionate presence in others' lives, always amenable to restoration and a new relationship with them, extending grace along the way in love.

Sometimes we may look for love in all the wrong places, mourning the loss of having a great father, a loving mother, doting grandparents for our children, or a close-knit, caring extended family that was never ours. We might think we could make those relationships happen, but we can't. All things are possible though Him who strengthens us and promises to always be with us through good times and bad. Love has been staring us in the face and moving into our hearts all our lives. We have a Father in heaven. He and His son Jesus love us deeply.

By forgiving, we can love through the perfect love that indwells each one of us, because of Jesus Christ. Here's how (Mark 11:22-25):

Jesus was matter-of-fact: "Embrace this God-life. Really embrace it, and nothing will be too much for you. This mountain, for instance: Just say, 'Go jump in the lake'—no shuffling or shilly-shallying—and it's as good as done. That's why I urge you to pray for absolutely everything, ranging from small to large. Include everything as you embrace this God-life, and you'll get God's everything. And when you assume the posture of prayer, remember that it's not all asking. If you have anything against someone, forgive—only then will your heavenly Father be inclined to also wipe your slate clean of sins.

There's always a way out of adverse situations. Think of a flickering candle placed far off in the unknown distance. Mysteriously shrouded in ominous gloom, hope is discovered even in the darkest days when we fervently search for it with our whole heart. Unwavering peace that is offered to all is found in Jesus Christ, Wonderful

Counselor, Lord, and Savior. Millions of people have been led to live a better life as they found healing and peace through Jesus.

I know all of this to be true because I have lived through challenging times myself. I can personally testify that Jesus Christ can bring you through any hardship you may now be facing or have ever experienced. Perhaps an impossible relationship has developed, an unspeakable act was perpetrated upon you, or grave difficulties are laying siege in your life. No matter how large or small your concerns may be, God cares about you and wants His best for you. He wants to bless you. His son Jesus has your back.

Jesus is the healer of broken hearts and wounded souls. He invites all to follow Him by simply saying, "Come." His invitation remains open to everyone. We're not alone in this life. He is always with us. God answers prayers by giving us what He knows we need. We generally find His perfect answer exceeds whatever we ask. Many times our prayers are answered in far more significant ways beyond our incredible imagination. Wherever you may find yourself at this moment in your spiritual journey, seek His healing power. As our heart cries out to Him, our tears on the altar signify a new beginning. He is always there waiting for us.

Forgiving in Real Life: Apply the Principles and Live these Truths — We always have Hope.
A Word Before You Go

We are never truly prayerless and never without hope. And we always have a choice. Our loving Father knows our heart, hears our silent cries, and is always with us.

You can feel rootless, disconnected, and disoriented in this crazy, topsy-turvy world. People of faith live daily in a state of unearned grace through God's mighty act of supreme sacrifice on our behalf, made in love. We may be free or actually suffer because of Jesus, but we will also live eternally because of Him ... and with Him.

Keep hope alive. Hope will always allow us to love forward. It's amazing what God can do in our lives when we forgive. Forgiveness is possible through Him. Through forgiveness, we free ourselves of the needless burdens we carry, allowing God to work in our life.

Philippians 4:7:

And the peace of God, which transcends all understanding, will guard your hearts and your minds in Christ Jesus.

THE LORD'S PRAYER

Our Father in heaven, Reveal who you are. Set the world right; Do what's best—
as above, so below.
Keep us alive with three square meals.
Keep us forgiven with you and forgiving others. Keep us safe from ourselves and the Devil. You're in charge!
You can do anything you want!
You're ablaze in beauty!
Yes. Yes. Yes.

ACKNOWLEDGMENTS

To many who know me, it seems I began writing this book a lifetime ago. I can unequivocally assure you that writing this book required a lifetime to create it. As with living life, it remains a work in progress.

I laugh, recalling a friend reminding me how writing a book takes a village. I feel exceptionally fortunate that mine has grown to immense proportions, blessing my endeavor. Thank you to my wonderful team of intercessors for your prayers for me and for this book.

To Reverend Greg Whitlock – Thank you for reviewing this book for theological soundness. May Jesus bless your time exponentially.

To Reverend David Brannock – Thank you for challenging me by setting the bar higher than I previously dared to dream ... keeping me on-course with your ongoing support for this book, in my long, slow-distance run to write it.

To Dr. Don Gordon – Thank you for your continued interest in my writing progress, amazing support, and enthusiastic encouragement in my seeing this book to completion.

To Reverend Matt Hearn – Thank you for your encouragement and prayers for this book.

To Andrea Merrell – I'm forever grateful for your dedication, encouragement, and expertise in helping to shape this book. Your perceptive editing and our friendship are a blessing!

To ten wonderful friends – Dana, David, Marcie, Norma, Don,

Frank, Susan, Ella, Terry, and Philip – Thank you for giving your time in considering and brainstorming book titles with me.

To my three beta reader teams – Thank you for your time and providing important feedback along this journey: David, Marcie, my Blue Ridge Mountains Christian Writers Conference 2018 Nonfiction Practicum Critique Partners, Carol, Stephanie, and Tillie. I pray blessings beyond measure.

To Debbie Haynes, Safe Harbor Founder – Thank you for adding your words about forgiveness, to open our conversation on this hard topic.

To my support team, all encouragers, and prayer warriors –thank you! Your tireless efforts sustained me in seeing this project through.

To my husband, family, and friends – I will never have enough words to express my heartfelt gratitude for all your incredible patience, immense understanding, and unfailing support you've poured over me.

To my children – I wish you all blessed lives filled to overflowing with true happiness, filled with unending joy and God's blessings. These three things you can count on: 1) God loves you (and all of us) more than we could ever know; 2) nothing will ever change how much I love you; 3) I am your Mom. Forever.

Heavenly Father, thank you for laying this important message (turned mission) on my heart. Thank you for preparing and teaching me all you have about forgiveness so I could tell others about it. Thank you for remaining steadfastly alongside me all the way through. I pray this book is pleasing to you. While my hope is this book will touch the lives and hearts of many for your glory, I am writing it for an Audience of One. AMEN.

ABOUT THE AUTHOR

BECKY CORTINO is a prolific writer and speaker whose words have appeared in a variety of publications as well as broadcast globally over every form of media. Her previous seven books are based on ministry she and her family participated in for over twenty years. Together, they served as pastoral care department ministry volunteers of a non-denominational hospital and in the children's care unit of a psychiatric hospital unit.

In the process of serving intergenerational groups, women, children, and families in this (and through her work in other ministries),

Becky observed an incredible range of human conditions. One of the greatest needs she saw was the shared need for improving relationships and resolving personal issues that hinder forgiving. She has experienced the challenges and blessings of forgiveness.

Becky Cortino is available for programs, presentations and podcast appearances.

More: BeckyCortino.com

Becky Cortino is also found on:

Facebook: facebook.com/BeckyCortino
Instagram: instagram.com/beckycortino
Twitter: twitter.com/BeckyCortino
Pinterest: pinterest.com/BeckyCortino
LinkedIn: linkedin.com/in/beckycortino
YouTube: youtube.com/BeckyCortino
Amazon: AmazonAuthor.BeckyCortino.org

#RestoringBrokenPlaces #ForgivenessBook

ALSO BY BECKY CORTINO

More Inspiration from Becky Cortino

Graphics/Memes with Quotes to Save and Share:
ForgivenessBkImages.BeckyCortino.org

Readers Speak - Ask Me Anything (AMA): Readers may submit questions about *Restoring the Broken Places,* share thoughts on the topic of forgiveness: ForgivBkReaders.BeckyCortino.org

What is Your Love Quotient? Take this Relationship Quiz and find out: LoveQuotientQuiz.LivRad.com

Receive "*9 Forgiveness Truths*" and Notes from Becky: AuthorSpeakerUpdates.BeckyCortino.org

***What is Your #1 Forgiveness Question/Concern/Challenge/Problem?* Submit yours (privately):** BeckyWantsToKnow.BeckyCortino.org

The Grace Daily Challenge Journal is designed to help readers and writers explore what the Bible says about grace and finding forgiveness, as they dig deep and journal, inspired by The Word: GraceDailyJournal.BeckyCortino.org

Encouraging Words for Hurting Hearts: LivRad.com

Becky Cortino is Available for Programs, Presentations, Podcasts: Book.BeckyCortino.info

Becky's Books and Media Available on Amazon:
AmazonAuthor.BeckyCortino.org

Becky's Creative Arts Ministry Books Available Directly from the Publisher: BeckyCortino.org

Before you go...

Please review this book on Amazon and Goodreads. It will give important feedback and help others find it.

Receive Special Reader Resources: Including Reader's Guide to this book, Forgiveness Bible Verse Guide and Bible Verse Cards, Forgiveness Inspirational Music Playlist and more Reader Perks by registering your book purchase here: ForgivenessBookResources.BeckyCortino.org

Made in the USA
Columbia, SC
20 July 2024